LETTER FROM THE KHYBER PASS

LETTER FROM THE KHYBER PASS

and other travel writing

GEORGE WOODCOCK

edited by Jim Christy

Douglas & McIntyre
Vancouver/Toronto

Copyright © 1993 by George Woodcock
Introduction copyright © 1993 by Jim Christy

93 94 95 96 97   5 4 3 2 1

All rights reserved. No part of this book may be reproduced or transmitted in any form by any means without permission in writing from the publisher, except by a reviewer, who may quote brief passages in a review.

Douglas & McIntyre
1615 Venables Street
Vancouver, British Columbia V5L 2H1

Canadian Cataloguing in Publication Data

Woodcock, George, 1912–
    Letter from the Khyber Pass and other travel writing

ISBN 1-55054-083-1
1. Woodcock, George, 1912–Journeys.   2. Authors, Canadian (English)—20th century—Journeys.*   I. Christy, Jim, 1945–
II. Title.
PS8545.O6Z53   1993   910.4   C93-091169-5
PR9199.3.W58Z475   1993

Editing by Barbara Pulling
Cover design by Tania Craan
Design by Rose Cowles
Typeset by The Typeworks
Printed and bound in Canada by D. W. Friesen & Sons Ltd.
Printed on acid-free paper

CONTENTS

INTRODUCTION
1

DON JAIME'S FIESTA
7

A DAY TO MITLA
13

PERU TODAY
23

A ROAD IN THE ANDES
27

CAMBODIA
36

LETTER FROM THE KHYBER PASS
47

THE EXCITING CENTRE OF THE MIDDLE EAST
51

A NORTHERN JOURNAL
57

LHASA IN THE JUNGLE
74

OASES IN A FLUID DESERT
83

SPIRIT DANCE OF THE SALISH PEOPLE
93

FROM ROTORUA TO TASMAN BAY
106

LOST WORLDS OF MEMORY
115

SEVEN BURMESE DAYS
131

ENCOUNTERS WITH INDIA
140

BACK TO SPAIN
158

THE CAVES IN THE DESERT
171

MY WORST JOURNEYS
190

FIRST FOREIGN LANDS
203

Introduction

> One rides out from Siem Reap
> along the straight jungle road
> with the metallic chorus of insects
> dinning in one's ears
> until the broad moat of Angkor Wat
> comes into sight, silvered
> by the lowering sunlight,
> with buffaloes wallowing
> ecstatically near the banks
> and wild duck feeding
> among the blossoming lotus.
>
> —from "Cambodia"

FIRST OF ALL, George Woodcock is probably the best writer of English prose around, and nowhere is this more evident than in his travel articles and essays. You can pick sentences almost at random from many of these pieces, break up the lines and arrange them, with no cheating, into verse that calls to mind the great nature mystics from Li Po to Kenneth Rexroth. Come to think of it, some of the satirical and political observations in these pieces would make good Catullus.

Woodcock maintains that his old friend George Orwell wrote a "crystalline, windowpane prose." The phrase describes his own prose just as well, but Woodcock has flung the windows of his writing open onto a much wider aspect. It would be difficult, in fact, to imagine any writer of our time who has broader interests and has covered more territory.

This statement will undoubtedly raise some hackles, cause other names to be invoked. Jan Morris, Paul Theroux and Peter Matthiessen may have called at more places, but the first two do little more than convey the surface aspects of the places they visit. Matthiessen alone of the three has human concerns, but he seems more interested in *people* than in individuals. His intellectual interests are intense but not nearly as extensive as Woodcock's, and what Matthiessen knows, he preaches. Woodcock is never tendentious. And he has what no one will ever accuse Matthiessen of possessing: a sense of humour.

As for range and breadth of learning, Woodcock has no peers among living writers. In recent times, only Ezra Pound, Herbert Read and Rexroth, also an autodidact, have displayed such intellectual voracity. But none of them were travellers.

Woodcock began as an imagist poet, but when he returned in the late 1940s to Canada, the country of his birth, he ceased for many years to write poetry. In British Columbia, forced to make a living by working with his hands, Woodcock encountered people who were new to him: Doukhobors and Indians, loggers, prospectors and all the characters of the West. The experience caused him to open up his writing style. Fortunately, he retained his imagist orientation, melding it with a new colloquial prose. The result is the windowpane prose so well displayed in these articles and essays.

Woodcock's output has been nothing less than phenomenal. Some take him for granted, like the weather. But there are many who regard him as a weathervane. As a young man, I was practically weaned on his anarchist writings: *Anarchism,* his survey of the modern movement, the biographies of Proudhon and Kropotkin, and his many pamphlets. Upon moving to Canada from the United States, I was pleased to discover that this was

Introduction

the same George Woodcock who was doing so much to make Canadian writers and literature better known. His readers in England might be surprised to know that the biographer of Orwell and Read, of Aldous Huxley, Oscar Wilde, William Godwin and Aphra Behn has also chronicled the lives of the Metis guerrilla leader Gabriel Dumont and early British Columbia newsman Amor De Cosmos, as well as producing a study of Northwest Coast Indian peoples and several books castigating the Canadian government.

Those familiar only with Woodcock, the historian, or Woodcock, the libertarian thinker, or Woodcock, the literary critic, might picture him as a fusty, V. S. Pritchett kind of literary tourist. But this would be a mistake. Woodcock is adventurous —and he is a romantic.

George Woodcock, a romantic? Most certainly, as you will see. In fact, as he wrote of another writer, he is among the last of the anarchistic romantics, "in love with freedom as the behaviour of men sometimes expresses it."

In this book, we see Woodcock wandering between the meridians by all manner of transport and encountering all sorts of people. He comes prepared but without prejudices or preconceived notions. He'll sample all the food and talk to anyone: a chief in Western Samoa, a teen-aged girl running a coffee shop in a Welsh mining town, a master carver at Rankin Inlet, a Canadian woman working with Tibetan refugees in the jungles of southern India, a Lebanese cab driver who invites him home for dinner and to meet the family. There are some splendid magic-realist snapshots in these travels—the way he sees Jaisalmer, for instance, after two days of crossing the Rajasthan desert, as a "vast mollusk lit by the late afternoon sun, with the spires of its nine Jain temples gleaming against the hard enamel-blue of the sky"; and his experience in a church at Mitla, where "the rows of dark draped figures seemed to flow forward like sombre waves, bearing the hundreds of points of light up to the altar where all the radiance broke in a golden surf over the glinting vessels and the copes of the priests and the great shining cliff of the retable with its saints in their bright and jewelled garments."

Woodcock gets into more than his share of scrapes, but this is bound to happen when one is curious and open to experience. We see him suffering from dysentery and being harassed by the Guardia Civil in Peru; the giant commandante, the tip of his scabbard scraping over the cobblestones, appears a comic opera bandito only when seen in the voyager's rearview mirror. Then there is the time he and his wife, Inge, are staying at a hotel in Chittagong, which Woodcock refers to as *rectum mundi*, being kept awake by mosquitoes, eating suspect food and using a "bathroom" that consists of a hole in the floor of the verandah; at the front door, the lepers wait. There are even some really hair-raising adventures here, in a small boat in a big storm off Western Samoa and on a bus careening down a tortuous Mexican mountain road, the driver so terrified he's crossing himself with his good hand and steering with his stump.

This is not a man breaking away from his desk and allowing himself to get into mischief for the sake of a good story. No, this is a writer who travels to replenish himself and who pursues his wanderings assiduously. No matter where he ventures, Woodcock is always working—which is not to suggest a single-minded scribbler intent on his notepad as he stumbles through native villages. Woodcock keeps his head up and his eyes and ears open, and gets the story by a kind of osmosis. Only later, in private, does he jot down his impressions.

His travel writing can be regarded as a compendium of wonders, with the information slipped between the lines. There is no hint of the lecturer here, yet we come away having learned something about the customs and ritual, the art and politics of the places and people Woodcock visits. He makes us *see*, too: the flora and fauna, the architecture, the faces of the people. All this and more is evident in the marvellous first paragraph of "Oases in a Fluid Desert," Woodcock's article about the Gilbert Islands. The piece itself is a masterly distillation of a book's worth of insight and observation.

Just as Woodcock has never been the conventional traveller, neither do his travel pieces adhere to the conventions of the genre. Some are straightforward accounts of what he saw, expe-

Introduction

rienced and reflected upon: "From Rotorua to Tasman Bay," for instance. In others, like "Cambodia," his own travels are implicit rather than directly described. Some of the essays and articles in this collection were written shortly after the experiences recounted, others decades later; some were composed from notes, some from memory. They are arranged chronologically, allowing us to witness not only the progression of a man through space and time but also the development of a style. And this arrangement enhances the elegiac power of the concluding pieces.

With a few exceptions, the articles and essays in this collection were originally published in journals and magazines. ("Lost Worlds of Memory" and "My Worst Journeys" appeared in anthologies, and the final essay, "First Foreign Lands," was written especially for this book.) Woodcock's book-length travel narratives, of which there are several, necessarily expand upon the material presented in many of these pieces, and the results, as interesting as they are, cannot avoid being weightier, the prose less flexible. The pictures of southern India, the South Seas, Mexico and Peru that we get here are not improved upon in his travel books. We see more of these places in the longer works, but we do not see them any better.

The most exotic of the experiences recounted in this book occurs not in the most far-flung place—the Khyber Pass, the Silk Road or an island west of Pago Pago—but closest to Woodcock's doorstep, in the Vancouver Island Indian village he calls Midden Bay, where he witnesses the Spirit Dance of the Salish people. But as Woodcock knows, one must venture to the ends of the earth to appreciate the marvellous in the neighbourhood.

Woodcock's travel writing makes us aware of a community of people throughout the world without rendering the world as in any way homogeneous. He pulls off what seems a conjuror's trick: simultaneously emphasizing our otherness, our uniqueness, while underscoring the connectedness of people everywhere.

When I think of meridians, I cannot help but picture actual lines upon the globe, and from there it does not require a great leap of the imagination to see those lines forming a cage. We are all trapped in this cage, wandering between the meridians, never so free as when longing to be free.

Woodcock here recounts a lifetime of travel and experience, often with such intensity of vision that those lines begin to blur and move, the cage becoming a wheel of fortune. The Wheel of Things, turning, turning...

Jim Christy

Don Jaime's Fiesta

1955

MEXICAN ANTICLERICALISM has been mostly an urban and a middle-class phenomenon, and the secularist campaign of President Calles, two decades ago, made little impression on the peasants or the people in most of the smaller towns. The Mexican countryman's occasional outbursts against the Church tend to be puritanical in character; he is impatient with the venality that has made the Mexican clergy a perpetually disreputable element in the Catholic world, but he clings obstinately to his own peculiar amalgam of Iberian Christianity and adapted paganism. Everywhere in Mexico, while the temporal power of the Church is almost destroyed, the social function of religion remains very strong.

A sign of this strength is the fact that in most places outside Mexico City the festivals of the Church consume more energy and devotion than the political festivals that the Republic has tried to erect in their place. I was particularly impressed by this fact during a recent period of residence in a small Central Mexican town where almost a score of churches and chapels have survived the vicissitudes of civil wars and secularist campaigns. Particularly in the poorer and more Indian parts of San Agustin, the church and its surrounding barrio form a social unit that is much more meaningful to the semi-illiterate people than the later municipal divisions, and the motive of prestige that plays so great a part in the Indian mind demands that every barrio should put forward a spectacular festival for its saint and its church. Indeed, it even becomes a question of personal and family prestige, for each year at each church one of the parishioners takes his turn as major-domo for the fiesta; he is responsible for arrangements and funds, and is supported by his relatives and his compadres, the men united to him in that most durable of all Mexican bonds—godfatherhood.

It happened that in the little barrio of La Salud, a district of artisans and labourers bordering on the market, Don Jaime, the cabinetmaker, was chosen as major-domo for the year of our visit. All Don Jaime's summer was dominated by the thought of the fiesta and, when we talked to him in his workshop, he would lament the old days when custom induced the head of every family to make his contribution. "Progress is never all one way, señor. We gain something like this"—and he patted the glistening new band saw he had just bought—"and we lose in responsibility." But it was evident that he was pleased with the honour his position would confer and really wished to share it only with his friends and his compadres.

As the day of the fiesta drew near, his preparations reached to every district of San Agustin. Walking among the poor streets towards the river, where the mosquitoes bite hard and the smell of sewage is habitual, we found Don Venustiano, the pyrotechnician, hard at work on his particular task. The sun had just set, and the light had that intense glow that precedes the rapid Mexican nightfall. The faded blues and yellows of the stuccoed walls burnt with a kind of inward luminosity that ignited the bright skirts of the girls who were drawing the night's water from the communal tap in the middle of the street and walking home with their red earthenware vases balanced on their shoulders. Don Venustiano, a mestizo craftsman who wore shoes instead of sandals, and jeans instead of the cotton pyjama trousers of his neighbours, worked in the failing light on the pavement outside his dark little doorway. His basic material was cane, which could be twisted into almost any shape and yet retain sufficient

Don Jaime's Fiesta

rigidity, and from this he constructed the units for his big set pieces. The gunpowder was supplied in an endless paper tube, which two boys in ragged baseball caps were fixing with cord to the frames. Don Venustiano was friendly but discreet: he was evasive about the ultimate purpose of his constructions; we would see them on the night of the fiesta, and then he was sure we would not be disappointed.

He was not the only craftsman preparing for Don Jaime's fiesta. In a workshop near the plaza a withered nonagenarian was working on the great paper lanterns that figure in every Mexican festival. Don Cherubino's person was as grimy as his shop. But his work, as he soldered the little tin holders for the candles and pasted his sheets of coloured tissue over their wire frames, was meticulously neat. Don Cherubino was neither polite nor instructive; he was of the old school who maintained an open dislike of gringos and made Rabelaisian comments about American women to the boys who collected in his shop.

By Saturday, activity on the fiesta had become generalized. Don Jaime's workshop was closed, and his compadres were neglecting their own businesses. Sounds of decoration and desultory cleaning came through the doors of La Salud, and electricians were fixing coloured lights around the great scallop shell of fluted sandstone that crowned its rococo façade. Marching music echoed in from the suburban outskirts, and a small procession wound in through the plaza. The Indian band, in white shirts and new sombreros, played a jaunty local tune with anarchic disregard of time, and behind them a score of youths carried a great wooden frame, forty feet long and six feet wide, covered with a trellis of cane interlaced with flowers. A second followed, and in the rear a lanky boy threw exploding firecrackers into the air as he walked. The frames were erected on either side of the entrance to La Salud; they were called *xochitl,* and this commemoration of an Aztec goddess was a hint of the pagan elements that linger in Mexican religion. During Saturday evening the poorer country people began to move into the market, with their burdens carried by tumplines around their brows. By the light of feeble naphtha flares they arranged their neat geometry of fruit for sale the next day—sharp-scented guavas and lumpy papayas and fresh-flavoured green oranges. They spent the night stretched out under their serapes on the cobbles.

With the first light of Sunday, the town was aroused by a salutation of firecrackers and a heavy tuneless clanging from the bell towers of all the churches, accompanied by the barking of a legion of lean dogs. As we went into the town, we were drawn towards La Salud by an obsessive piping; a solitary musician—the *chirimetero*—was standing in a niche beside the door, playing on pipe and tabor an ancient theme, which he repeated for hours on end throughout the day. The Indians streamed past him into the church, praying to a tortured Christ bleeding with realistic gore before a vast gilded retable that was decorated with banked lilies and with lengths of scarlet satin hanging down from the faded heaven of the broad-arched vault. All day long the services went on in relays, and priests in gilded copes administered the Host to worshippers of whom many were literally dressed in rags. As it was a fiesta, the Sunday market was unusually large; potters, serape weavers and sandal makers had come in from the surrounding towns, and there were sellers of religious pictures and yellow wax candles and ballads. Along the crowded walk behind the market, Indian women cooked malodorous stews of entrails and lungs over charcoal braziers; their customers squatted on the pavement's edge, deftly using their tortillas as spoons. Village healers traded with the herbalist for specifics they could not find locally. There were vendors of rush mats from Chapala, and sombreros from Michoacán, and ropes of maguey fibre from Querétaro.

The marketplace was the headquarters of the country people, but out in the plaza the townsfolk also were in festival mood. The mestizo band played "Poet and Peasant" and "La Paloma" as the youths and girls walked in opposing circles around the fountains. Shoeblacks did a roaring trade with shop assistants who were showing off the Cuban-heeled high boots that are the prevalent fashion in this part of Mexico. And in a corner by the *Municipio,* Don Cherubino, rejuvenated by excitement, let up fire balloons of coloured paper that bore far into the sky the advertisements of "Doble Cola," the local rival of the drink that symbolizes gringo imperialism. Siesta time, between two and

Don Jaime's Fiesta

four, brought a weakening of activity. The townspeople went home to rest, the rancheros dozed on church benches or sat under the trees munching tacos and drinking milky pulque. And in the evening activity was concentrated around the crowded floodlit façade of La Salud. From our perch on the steps of the market the crowded sombreros looked like a field of enormous mushrooms, contrasting with the dark shawls under which the girls and women shaded their delicate, almost Malayan faces. The noise was immense. The two brass bands performed alternately, but the mariachi guitarists among the crowd never seemed to cease their sombre plateau tunes—Castilian melancholy overlaid with Indian resignation—and often, above the other sounds, we would hear the great voice of the ballad singer, Blind José, echoing from the cantino El Vampiro down the street.

The most remarkable aspect of this scene was the apparent autonomy of its various activities. The performers did not appear very much aware of each other or even of their audiences, while the latter were the perfect passive spectators, silent and good-humoured. But the most self-absorbed of all were the *concheros* —members of the Indian dancing guilds. Hour after hour they trod their stylized patterns on the cobbles before the church, crowns of coloured plumes swaying as they bowed and capered, cloaks of brilliant satin swirling as they beat their heraldic shields and wooden swords in formal re-enactment of the Conquest, shell-encrusted leggings jingling in time with the tiny armadillo-shell mandolins of their leaders. At ten o'clock the concheros entered the church in full procession, with their banners of the Crucifixion carried before them. We squeezed in through the door as they danced, with guitars thrumming and rattles beating, to the flowered altar, where they formed an agitated line of colour and movement, the Aztec geometry of their shields and cloaks contrasting with the baroque imagery around them. Banners dipped and feet stamped in rhythms that once worshipped Quetzalcotl as they sang their shrill chant to the Virgin of Guadalupe, patron of the Indians. It was a moving irruption from the past, and the priest seemed uneasy as he hurriedly distributed his wafers among the dancers.

Then came, outside the church, the pyrotechnic finale. First, Don Venustiano deployed his army of mobile pieces. Angels blazed down in glory on ropes from the bell tower. Flaming alligators of painted paper darted on catherine wheels among the crowd. Bulls snorted fire and burnt serapes and rebozos as excited youths swung them on poles over our heads. Finally, there was Don Venustiano's masterpiece, the *castillo*. It was a good castillo, for no fewer than ten tiers of framework were attached to the forty-foot pole let down into the middle of the street. Don Venustiano deliberately lit the fuse for the bottom tier; in an instant it burst into a maze of whirling wheels and jets of green and red and gold; the fire ran on a pilot fuse to the next tier, and so on, each level burning separately until, at the tip of the pole, plaster angels span round a dizzy globe of fire and the flag of Mexico broke out in patriotic triumph. The mestizos exclaimed with delight, the Indians grinned. La Salud had held its own against the rival barrios. Don Jaime's fiesta was ended.

A Day to Mitla

1955

OUR THIRD DAY at Oaxaca was marked by one of those unpremeditated incidents that so often excel in quality and meaning the planned experiences on whose fulfillment they impinge.

Oaxaca is one of the few Mexican towns whose people have taken advantage of the climate and the arcaded plazas to adopt the Latin custom of eating out of doors. On a *terrasse* in the zócalo a girl with a bony Mayan face—the sloping brow and large Hittite nose of the Palenque temples—brought our breakfast of cinnamon-flavoured chocolate and sweet rolls. For a while we watched the knife sellers from Ejutla carefully burnishing their blades in the garden opposite before starting the day's peddling. Then a tall young man from Georgia strolled up to our table and, regardless of the score of Americans who sat within hearing distance, drawled out: "Ain't it fahn to git away from all those damned tourists in Puebla?" Coyly he searched in his shirt pocket and then unwrapped a screw of tissue paper to show us a couple of Maximilian coins that he was going to have made into earrings for his girl in Nashville. "Ah'm gettin' down to Salina Cruz—still too many goddamned tourists," he concluded.

A Zapotec woman dangling filigree pendants out of her basket took his place; they were authentically handmade and solid yellow gold, but they had that excessive slickness of design that would have fitted them admirably for a five-and-ten store, and they reminded us once again of the suicidal vulgarity of taste by which the Mexican craftsman too often tries to compete with the mass-produced junk that is driving him out of business. We went through all the lengthy Mexican procedure of explaining that our lack of interest was not just the basis for a spell of bargaining and then, as the woman passed to the next table, we decided to leave before the morning rush of shoeblacks and serape sellers, and to spend the day out at the temples of Mitla, twenty miles away.

We canvassed the taximen who drowsed in their cabs under the plane trees around the corner in the Alameda. They were urbanized mestizos who had risen above bargaining and stuck fast to their cartel rate of sixty pesos, as against a return fare of seven pesos on the bus. We turned away and walked past the heavy baroque block of the cathedral and the balconied stone buildings of the main streets towards the market and the bus station beyond. The centre of Oaxaca is built of a grey stone that is faintly suffused with green. Travellers have made much of this greenness but, except at that hour of sunset when all the subdued colours of Mexico take on a preternatural intensity, it is not very evident, and as we walked past in the morning sunlight all we could see was the subtlest suggestion of a soft young-almond shade.

Even though it was not market day, the marketplace and the streets around it were full of vendors and of Oaxacan housewives going about their morning shopping. A train of donkeys trotted across our path, bearing rope nets filled with round black water pots from San Bartolo Coyetepec, pots with a faint greyish bloom that made them look like vast jetty grapes. Other donkeys carried tall, cylindrical baskets filled with chilis or corn cobs, while sombreroed boys rode bareback astride their rumps —the only place to avoid a burro's knobbly vertebrae.

In the trading area, the cobbles were laid out with rush mats on which the Indian women sat and displayed their goods. A rough pattern of lanes had been observed, but these were very narrow, and a couple of townswomen bargaining with the vendors would create a block that had to be skirted very carefully to avoid treading on the merchandise.

Around Oaxaca there are many more unhispanicized Indians than one sees in northern Mexico, and a number of tribes were represented in the market—Zapotecs and Mixtecs, Mixes and Chinantecs. Instead of clinging to the faded cotton dresses and sooty grey shawls that have become almost a uniform for poor women in the north, the Oaxaca country people tend to reproduce their variety of culture in their dress. We saw some wearing bright and heavily pleated skirts with embroidered white bodices, and others with rough, handwoven skirts consisting each of a rectangular piece of cloth folded around the waist and held in place by a bright red sash. Yet others had extremely full skirts of rough white linen, with loose, hooded smocks that made them look like burnoosed Arabs at a short distance, and two handsome Tehuanas strutted among the crowd in the flowered dresses and loose *huipil* blouses of the isthmus. There was just as much variety of headdress. Some still used the dim shawl, or rebozo, but instead of draping it over the head like a Lancashire mill woman, as is done in the north, they would either coil it into a complicated turban or hang it freely over the shoulder to display their hair plaited with red or purple ribbons. Others again wore a white folded napkin perched on top of the head, with a tilt over the brow, almost like a limp mortarboard. The faces of these women were more rounded than those of the Aztecs, and paler, ranging over the ivories towards a milky coffee colour.

The mats on which they sat—gossiping, laughing with a freedom one rarely sees among the reserved plateau Indians, meticulously delousing their children's hair and occasionally selling a few centavos' worth of goods—carried neat piles of fruits and vegetables, by some mutual consent arranged according to kind. A few yards of purplish onions, a few yards of bulky green papayas, a few yards of crimson chilis. Piles of mottled green Mexican oranges, commercially so unattractive and in taste so delectable, alternated with fat sprays of gigantic cooking plantains and little stubby paws of red eating bananas. There were piles of terracotta pomegranates and of zapates, a fruit that looks like a green persimmon and is eaten when its rotten interior has become a black paste that is mashed with lemon juice into one of the best Mexican sweets.

We finally pushed our way out of this crowded area and, after passing a few mats where women were selling small dried fish that looked like carp, and some trays of cheap cosmetics that their mestizo proprietors had decorated with sprays of white orchids, we found the Mitla bus, already half full of Zapotec farmers, some clad modernly in blue jeans and Panama hats, others in the old-fashioned pyjama suits of white cotton. The top was loaded with bundles and bags and baskets, and then the Indian driver, whose squat figure and sombre face gave him a surprising resemblance to Juarez, climbed into his seat, turned on the radio, which blared out a tune from *Limelight* that has become a Mexican hit, and began to drive out through the narrow streets behind the market and towards the wide highroad that leads out to Tehuantepec and the Guatemalan border.

This road passes down a valley with arid clay-yellow hills on either side, scantily dotted with desiccated bushes; we amused ourselves by speculating which of the more conical of these eminences might be unexcavated pyramids or might at least contain some unexplored temple precinct like Monte Albán. In the valley there were fields of peanuts, and slender castor-oil bushes, with splayed reddish leaves and fuzzy bunches of fruit, and the small bluish century plants from which mescal is made. Donkeys and goats grazed on yellow-looking meadows, and once we passed a flock of at least twenty vultures dipping their scrawny necks and funereally dingy bodies over some pleasant scavenging task. The peasants on the bus talked gutturally in Zapotec, and a girl on the seat before us read an article headed *"El Dominio de Rey Muerte"*—The Dominion of the King of Death. When she turned over the pages of her magazine I realized that it was a Spanish-language publication of the Jehovah's Witnesses.

We passed through several small villages of dusty-looking adobe huts, and then turned off the main road into a small town. Most of the buildings were still mud brick, with orange trees in their gardens and purple bougainvillaeas flaming over their garden walls, but a few stone houses and some small, cavernous shops surrounded the little jacaranda-shaded plaza. On some of the heavy doors opening on to the courtyards of houses there were little placards bearing the motto, *Viva el Cristo Rey*—this time meaning Long Live Christ the King. It was evident that we were in an unusually religious town for this part of Mexico.

As the bus stopped in the plaza, a young man in city clothes came back and told us that there was to be a twenty minutes' stop and that the driver had told him the church was worth seeing. We had already seen dozens of churches up and down Mexico, and it was rather with the thought of filling in the time of our stop than in the hope of finding anything interesting that we agreed to accompany him. As we walked across the sandy space before the church, whose barrenness was relieved only by the white trumpets of a large *casaguate* tree, our companion told us that he was an Argentinian who had been an exchange student in the United States and was now making his way southward and taking in as much of Latin America as he could on his way. Mexico shocked him; in his country, he assured us, there was nothing like the same disparity between the rich and the poor.

Except for its unusual loftiness in what seemed a rather small town, the church's façade was not exceptional; it was in the rather solid Oaxacan version of the richly carved Mexican baroque. Only when we stood in the shade of the open doorway did our idly conceived experience assume sudden meaning and uniqueness. The interior was high-vaulted, and its stone, uncoated by plaster, was painted in a blue that had faded into a pale cerulean—the colour of a far-receding Northern sky rather than the deeper and closer blue of Mexico—and this, in combination with the enormous and ornately carved and gilded retable behind the altar, seemed to extend the dimensions of the church to a cathedral-like immensity. It was packed to the door with kneeling Indians; towards the front on the left-hand side was a solid square of men and boys in white shirts, but the rest of the nave was filled with women and girls, who must have outnumbered the men by more than three to one. They wore their rebozos, which out of the sunlight appeared dead black, over their heads and shoulders, and each held a burning candle in her left hand. The rows of dark draped figures seemed to flow forward like sombre waves, bearing the hundreds of points of light up to the altar where all the radiance broke in a golden surf over the glinting vessels and the copes of the priests and the great shining cliff of the retable with its saints in their bright and jewelled garments. Of that tide the sound was given by a little string band of elderly Indians at the side of the church. I cannot remember what—or even what kind of—music they were playing, and having heard Indian instrumentalists before and since I can imagine they were probably very bad, but in that moment of feeling as we looked up the church and were caught in the flood of faith that seemed to flow like a steady current afterwards, it sounded as spiritual and austere as Bach. Hitherto, when I had gone into Indian churches and had seen the peasants praying with their arms held cruciformly, I had felt an intruder and had padded softly away, but here, in a feeling that included but went far beyond the aesthetic, there was a sudden and basically inexpressible sense of illumination and fellowship.

The showpiece of this church was a side chapel into which we went afterwards; its walls and ceilings were completely covered with carved moldings of wood, in sinuous, organic shapes, which had been coated with gilded gesso, now either tarnished or chipped to reveal the original wood. Some of the glow of gold remained, richer with the darkening of age, but the sense of grain and growth also came through. For a moment I thought that these freely curving forms were alien to the native Indian art, but then I remembered the Zapotec reliefs called The Dancers up in Monte Albán, above Oaxaca, and realized that these flowing forms were merely a development of the same art in another medium and another cause. Outside the chapel, under the *casaguate* tree, a young woman with heavy crescent earrings of pale gold told us that the town was called Tlacolula.

Mitla lies seven miles on. The Zapotecs used to call it the "earth-strong pueblo," and I have never seen a town that looked more akin to the ground on which it stood. Almost all the houses in the present-day settlement were built of adobe bricks of exactly the same orange-sandy colour as the dusty earth of

A Day to Mitla

the yards and the side streets. They were fenced with tall hedges of organ cactus, sombre green and impenetrable, and only towards the centre of the town did a few tiled roofs relieve the feeling that one was entering a troglodytic village in which the homes, with their drab reed thatches, were merely extensions of some underground city. In the centre there had been a shoddy intrusion of modernism; a kind of steel Dutch barn served as a market hall, and a few stores and cantinas had been plastered and painted over with gaudy advertisements of beer—Cerveza Moctezuma and Cerveza Bohemia.

We took the stony road out of the square towards the ruins. An old man in a white suit walked before us, and the village women kissed his hands in respect as they met him. Two small boys attached themselves, told us that they never went to school and insisted on leading us over the ford and up the slight hill to the wide grey temples and the big Spanish church that had been built among them to take over the reverence with which the Indians had regarded the site.

To the Zapotecs, Mitla is the middle of the earth—*mitad del mundo;* it is also the city of souls. Here the ancient Zapotec kings of the valley are said to have been buried, and here all the spirits of good members of the tribe are still said to gather after they are dead. But not much of the reverence one might have expected towards such a sacred place was shown by the living Zapotecas we met at the ruins, for we had barely walked out on to the grassy area before the long walls of the courtyards when a crowd of girls and women rushed forward from the fountain where they had been sitting and began to wave pebble necklaces before our faces and to ring in our ears the black pottery bells from San Bartolo that chime as clear and true as any metal. They even had little clay images that looked quite authentic—until three women held up three identical figures!

A young man with the wide, almost Tibetan face of the Mitlans took us in hand as the official guide. Following his lead, we admired the cyclopean structure of the buildings, with their exact masonry, their enormous architrave blocks raised without cranes and the neat mosaic stonework decorations that make the site unique. We ducked into tombs and crawled on our knees, carrying candles in our hands, into underground chambers that were as hot as deep mines, in order to see delicate paintings of the gods on the remnants of red stucco that clung to the walls.

Enough has been written about Mitla by archaeological experts to make it unnecessary for me to record more than a fleeting impression. But one thing seems worth mentioning. Much has been made of the textilelike patterns of the mosaic designs; some have called them "frozen lace," and Aldous Huxley, misled by the presence of local serapes in the same patterns, went so far as to suggest that the masons had copied from the weavers. I would dissent from this; it seems to be established that the use of the Mitla patterns in blankets is recent and, from what I could see, they seem excellently adapted to the mosaic technique that was used by the temple builders.

Except for the mosaics and some fragments of painting, I found the Mitla temples disappointing. They lacked the magnificent hilltop setting of Monte Albán, the panoramic planning of the Toltec ceremonial city at Teotihuacán. And perhaps, also, they suffered a disadvantage because we were fresh from our experience of a more living and therefore meaningful aspect of religious ritual at Tlacolula.

After we had left the temples, we went into the empty whitewashed church beside them. It had a retable almost as fine as that in Tlacolula, and there were some handsome saints that the villagers had decorated with white and rose-coloured orchids. As we stood there, the cracked bell began to toll over our heads, and the guide crossed himself and said that someone had died in Mitla. We went out and climbed an adobe pyramid on the other side of the road; a seventeenth-century Spanish chapel had been built on it, so starkly constructed of bricks that it looked like a Victorian railway halt. Around its walls the ants had been excavating the pyramid, and the entrances to their nests were ringed with glittering piles of tiny rock crystals that they had brought out from the labyrinthine passages of their nests.

Back in the plaza we had to wait for a bus and filled the time by lunching at the only clean-looking restaurant. It was kept by a blond Swiss, the son of an immigrant, and when we told him

A Day to Mitla

that we had spent many months at Thun and Zermatt and Basel, he treated us to glasses of mellow mescal and sat at our table with his Spanish wife to talk of the fatherland he had never seen, and to worry, like any burgher of Zurich, about the prospect of war. He and an American woman who kept a curio shop opposite were almost the only non-Zapotecs in Mitla. The natives, being great travellers themselves, are tolerant to strangers, and the main rifts seemed to be within the tiny foreign community, for the American woman, whom we met shortly afterwards, complained acidly about the decorations of the Swiss restaurant, which were indeed a little gaudy, and remarked darkly that every week *somebody* came out and cut off the shoots of the bougainvillaeas she had planted along the front of her porch.

The bus back was largely filled with sturdy, grubby women from the mountain hamlets above Mitla, who tramped down, carrying on their backs enormous bundles that were held by tumplines across their chests. They wore bright blue pleated skirts and had red cords braided into their long black hair; their linen blouses were cut so low under the arms that their sagging brown breasts were visible from the side as they walked.

The driver on this run was a mestizo from the city, and he appeared with his girl friend, a kind of Latin Marilyn Monroe who seemed about to burst in every direction of bosom and buttock from the tight silk dress she wore. Not merely did she make a show of her body, which no Indian woman would have done but, ignoring the notices not to disturb the driver, she sat beside him and lavished caresses on him of a kind one rarely sees in Mexico, where even a public kiss is unusual. The Indians watched in silent disapproval, not even reacting when the woman's wriggling weight collapsed the folding seat on which she had placed herself and precipitated her to the floor of the bus. Then the engine broke down, and the driver did not have the necessary tools to adjust it. We stood about in the road until he could borrow them from a long-distance lorry driver. Even then, he could do very little, and we eventually crawled slowly, at burro pace, into Oaxaca. There the setting sun was at last lighting up the green of the buildings. Thousands of black screaming birds jostled in the trees of the main plaza, where the government officials with sleek Castilian faces bent over their evening games of dominoes outside the Marques del Valle Hotel, and the descendants of the Zapotec warriors whacked out "Jalisco" on their marimbas among the gingerbread ironwork of the little bandstand.

Peru Today

1956

THE LAST STOP on the way from Vancouver to Lima was at Guayaquil, in Ecuador, where the CPA flights from Mexico City put down for refuelling. A warm wind swayed the palm trees and the hibiscus bushes, and out in the darkness, beyond the range of the airport lights, sang a strident chorus of treefrogs and crickets.

"Welcome to Guayaquil, 132 miles south of the Equator," read a notice in English, and the waiting room had a feeling of seedy friendliness as its officials idled around with an air of not caring in the least whether one of the passengers might decide to make an unauthorized break for the interior. The lean Negro selling Panama hats, the woman with grey bobbed hair behind the refreshment bar who looked as though she might have kept a general store in an English village—one had the feeling that the tropics was running true to the type established by a generation of English novelists.

Lima was still well within the tropics, but the change was startling, even when one had already been told of the city's climatic eccentricities. A pallid grey mist hung in the sky when we arrived—and stayed there throughout the months we remained in Peru. There was no rain, but on our first evening a clammy drizzle began to fall, and the air was so chilly that we shuddered in tweed jackets and looked with understanding at the smart Lima women in their overcoats and woollen suits, at twelve degrees below the equator.

Lima's climate is determined by an ocean current, which keeps the rain clouds away from the Peruvian coast and yet, by creating its own mist—*La Garua,* the Lima people call it—makes the climate cool in winter and not very hot in summer. Because of the lack of rain, the whole coast from the Ecuadorian to the Chilean border is a long desert that reaches up into the western foothills of the Andes and is broken only by the green streaks of infrequent river valleys. Lima lies on one of these rivers, the Rímac, but on every side, except up the valley, the desert creeps to the very edge of the city.

Lima is a city whose charm is not obvious or immediate, like that of some other Peruvian cities, such as Arequipa and Cuzco. To taste the real flavour of the City of Kings, as Pizarro named it, one has to linger there, to watch the leisured life of the people, and to observe the variety of their types—aristocrats of the purest Spanish extraction and women with clear olive skins and that slim-waisted hourglass figure that is so much appreciated by Peruvians, Indians in the vivid native costumes of the Andes and gypsies in pavement-sweeping skirts of gaudy silk, Negro street vendors and Italian storekeepers, English engineers and Cantonese cooks, whose restaurants play a great part in Peruvian life.

In time, we found that it was a city of odd and unexpected pleasures, of little hidden squares and gardens, of flowery Andalusian patios and Spanish mansions with screened wooden balconies in the Moorish style, of elegant eighteenth-century palaces hidden among the slums, like that of La Perricholi (the half-breed actress who became a viceroy's mistress and the heroine of *The Bridge of San Luis Rey*), and of curious colonial churches like San Francisco, where the brown-robed friars took us into rambling catacombs inhabited by flitting bats and filled with the bones of twelve thousand people, arranged with macabre ingenuity in symmetrical piles and patterns.

The City of Kings can best be enjoyed by those with well-filled purses. One day I had to visit a Canadian banker who was working in Lima, and after we had finished our business, he said: "I hope that when you go back you will not write, as some people have done, that living is cheap in Lima." The only reasonably good hotels in the centre of Lima are not cheap ($9.00 or more for a double room), and it is hard to get a good meal in the capital for much less than $2.50. These prices reflect the high cost of living among the middle class, i.e., among those who buy any quantity of the manufactured or processed goods that have to be imported, since Peru has very little industry above the primary levels of agriculture or mining.

Beyond its old Spanish centre, Lima has spread in recent years into a wide periphery of suburbs that stretch out towards the sea; very soon they will unite the capital with the rowdy, busy old seaport town of Callao. It is in these suburbs, with their wide boulevards and brilliant gardens and the glittering supermarkets that have recently been introduced, that the prosperous people of Lima live, and the houses they have built themselves make a jumbled museum of styles, from Spanish colonial and Moorish, Gothic and Tudor to modernistic imitations of Le Corbusier and the Bauhaus school. The modernistic element has also entered into the new public buildings that have been built in the centre of Lima, such as the Ministry of Education and the palatial Social Security Hospital, but Peruvian architects handle the contemporary idioms with unsure hands, and they have produced nothing to compare with the best of Mexico or Brazil.

The fact that Lima should have spread towards the sea rather than towards the mountains is in some ways symbolic of the outlook of its people. Peru is divided geographically into three clearly defined regions—the long western desert of the coast, the sierra of high plateaus and valleys embraced by the various ranges of the Andes, and the jungle that slopes down on the east towards the Amazon. Lima is much more conscious of the world beyond its frontiers than it is of the regions beyond the nearest mountain range; on the other hand, it is united by economic interest and also by the Pan-American highway (Peru's single important paved road), with the coastal regions to both the north and south.

We travelled along the Pan-American highway for a thousand miles of its length, proceeding mostly by *collectivo,* a kind of long-distance taxi in which each of the five passengers pays for a single seat. Hour on hour we would speed through the stark and awesome monotony of the desert—a desert so barren that those scattered regions where a few cacti or squat carob trees grew seemed positively fertile in contrast to the rest. One felt as relieved as a Bedouin traveller to see the green of one of the rare valleys, which provided their narrow oases of sugar cane fields and banana plantations dotted by primitive *chozas,* or Indian huts of cane plastered with mud.

On this coastline, scattered through the desert, we found some of the most progressive towns of Peru and also some of its most remarkable archaeological sites. Around Trujillo, in the days before the Inca empire, the Chimu civilization flourished, and one day we went with an archaeological student to visit the remains of the great city of Chan Chan, which was once its capital. For miles on each side of the Pan-American highway stretched the high, tawny adobe walls of this ancient community, which at its height must have sheltered almost 200,000 inhabitants; they were a people who made exquisite ceramics and woven materials, who understood the arts of surgery and smelting, and devised great irrigation systems to tame the desert.

Within the limits of their Bronze Age culture, the Chimu appear to have solved very capably the problems of living in the harsh environment of the Peruvian coast, and it seemed appropriate when, in this same region, we came across the symptoms of an attempt to create a similar reconciliation of man and nature in modern terms. For it is in the old Chimu kingdom, through such projects as the oil refineries of Talara, the steel plants of Chimbote and the power stations of the Santos valley, that the developments that will give Peru a more balanced industrial life are growing up on the edge of the desert, often in the very shadow of the temples and fortresses of the vanished Indian civilizations.

A Road in the Andes

1957

DOWN THROUGH the long coastal desert of Peru, from the border of Ecuador to the border of Chile, runs the long asphalted ribbon of the Pan-American highway. Cutting through the vast dead city of Chan Chan and running in the shadow of pre-Inca Pachácamac, passing the orange groves of Nazca and the sugar fields of Ica, linking the ancient northern city of Trujillo (traditional centre of liberal revolutions) with the ancient southern city of Arequipa (traditional centre of military coups), it gives a unity to the Peruvian seaboard that the rest of that country of mountain and jungle has not yet achieved.

It is also, with one small exception, the only fully paved highway in Peru. The exception, which is in a way the subject of these notes, is a short stretch of thirty miles of road that runs from a comparatively small mining town in the Andes to an even smaller market town. The mining town is La Oroya, the market town is Tarma, and they, and the road that links them, epitomize rather dramatically some of the characteristic and—to many strangers—disquieting aspects of Peruvian social life.

We first saw La Oroya on our journey from Lima into the western Andes. The Central Railway of Peru clambers on multiple switchbacks up the steep mountainsides and crawls through the high, bare valleys of the range until, almost sixteen thousand feet above the sea, it crosses the Continental Divide and dips into the valley of the Mantaro. La Oroya lies some three thousand feet below the pass, in a wide bowl where the high black chimneys of its smelters stand dramatically against twisted limestone crags whose marmoreal pallor led the local Indians to call them the Hills of the Moon.

I have never been in Johannesburg, but my imaginary picture of that city is dominated—on a larger scale, of course—by the same mixture of industrialism and primitivism as one encounters on entering La Oroya. At first all one sees of the town are the great sooty mine buildings and the long lines of rough brick dwellings where the workers live; these are little more than cubicles, each with a small kitchen at the back and in the front a single room where the whole family camp, usually without the mediation of a bed between them and the floor. I use the word "camp" deliberately, for there is a pervadingly transient air about life in La Oroya. The miners are mostly Quechua Indians from the surrounding sierra—descendants of the Incas' subjects, and even in the industrial environment they live almost as if they had never left their native valleys. Wearing the brilliant multiple skirts of colonial days, the women cook in earthenware pots—preferably in the open—the stodgy potato soup called *chupe* that has been an Andean staple since the days before history. They shop in little markets where the medicine woman and the coca seller do as good a trade as they would in any remote village that had never seen a doctor. Even the music that screams from the loudspeakers in the hole-in-the-wall eating houses is mountain music, with *chola* women chanting harshly to the resonant beat of deep-bellied harps and the screech of *quenas*.

Like most Peruvian mining centres, La Oroya was founded by the Spaniards, and on the hill above the modern settlement the battered but graceful wooden-balconied houses of colonial days still overhang the narrow streets that smell of urine and *ají*. Red-cheeked half-breed girls stand in the doorways selling *chica*, the cloudy brown maize beer, and barefooted boys fly kites in the shabby plazas.

But the worlds of Indian peasantry, of Spanish colonial town life, of a delayed industrial revolution making its own little Black Country among the mountains—these are not the only aspects of La Oroya. There is a fourth life that in a sense presides over them all and unites them into the curious amalgam that makes the town typical of so much in modern Peruvian life.

The old Spanish town and the long ranks of miners' hovels are all on one side of the Mantaro, which at this point has scooped itself a deep gorge with precipitous rock sides. Over the river, and enclosed at the rear by tall cliffs, lies a suburb of bungalows that are inhabited by the engineers and officials of the mining corporation. Most of them, like their company, are American, and they and their families carry on a life whose detachment from that of the Indians they employ is both assured and symbolized by the bridge that is the only way across the gorge; it is guarded constantly by armed men, and no one is allowed to cross without a pass.

La Oroya, indeed, is a living example of a quasi-colonial past that is on its way out in most other parts of Latin America; in Peru it survives, and this settlement of American technicians, living a very similar life to that of English officials in the old India, is an indication of the power that foreign capital still holds in the Andes. American, English and German corporations control not only the railways, the internal airways and most of the large-scale mining in Peru, but also several of the important banks and much of the sugar industry. Revolutions flare up, governments change, dictators rise and depart, as General Odria departed during the early weeks of our visit to Peru, but in this ballet of the Ins and Outs the economic power of the foreign corporations has suffered surprisingly little diminution.

This situation is linked closely with the general social backwardness of Peru. Its one permanently effective revolution was the independence movement of the early nineteenth century; this transferred power from the Spanish-born military and official caste to the creole gentry, and power still remains to all intents and purposes in the uneasy alliance between landlords, generals and foreign companies. Since there is only a small middle class, liberal movements have been weak, particularly as they have gained almost no support from the peasants of the Andes who withdrew from anything resembling political interests after the defeat of the Indian rebellion under Tupac Amaru in the 1780s. Nothing resembling the Mexican agrarian revolution has ever taken place in Peru, and the hacienda system carries on very much as it did a hundred years ago; in some regions the labourers on the great latifundia still work for fifteen cents a day plus a food allowance that consists of little more than maize and potatoes. Illiteracy is common, and among the peasants of the sierra it is the rule rather than the exception; as only those who write can vote, this means that the majority of poorer Peruvians are disenfranchised.

These facts are the background to some of the oddities of Peruvian political life, and they in turn take us back to La Oroya and to that magnificently engineered road that runs from there down through the mountains to Tarma. By the time we made this trip we had already seen a good deal of the Andes and of the bad gravel and dirt roads that link the shabby and often decrepit highland towns. The Tarma road was therefore something of a surprise as, starting out from the station at La Oroya, it climbed, smooth and wide, into the bare mountaintop pastures, where the grazing llamas raised their long necks and eyed us with the disdainful glances of transmigrated dowagers. Later it descended into the valley where Tarma lay; the slopes of the mountains were patterned brilliantly with the yellow and green and orange of the "hanging fields," those farms at improbably steep angles that are tilled by the Indian communes forced out of the rich valley bottoms by the Spaniards. Our neighbour on the bus pointed out a ribbon of grey stone tracing its way along the opposite hillside and then passing under the modern highway and disappearing into a narrow break in the rocks. "It is the Inca road," he said. "Once it was the great military way from Quito to Bolivia, and the Indians still use it for their pack trains of llamas."

A Road in the Andes

Eventually Tarma came into sight far below as we careened down the hairpin bends. The width of the road had led us to expect a large city. Instead, as we saw it clustering in the valley, we realized that Tarma was small, and pleasant as these sierra towns go; the white stuccoed houses that clambered up the hillsides among the eucalyptus groves gave it a frail suggestion of Tuscany.

However, we soon learned that it was not merely the road to Tarma that was remarkable, for as we walked through the town's modest streets we passed more new and ambitious buildings than we had seen anywhere else in Peru; a massive and ornate cathedral glittered over the little plaza, a large hospital stood ready for some general to open with formal pomp, a finely designed market hall was being completed and two new schools had just been put into operation.

How, in a country where relatively little money filters through the public financial system to construction projects, had such a small town come to be so grandly favoured? We put the question to a young Peruvian engineer whom we met in the bar of the Government Hotel.

"It is all very simple," he said. "You have heard of General Odria, our late president? Well, there you have your explanation. Odria was a native of Tarma. He went away as a little barefooted *cholito,* and he came back as a dictator, resolved to do everything he could for his home town. That, incidentally, is why you find this hotel so good. Odria built it for his own pleasure. And while he was in power it was often very uncomfortable to be staying here, for as soon as the president wanted to take a holiday, all the guests would be turned out, and Odria would come up on his special train to La Oroya. Then he would drive down on that fine new road, and he and his guards would take over the hotel. You noticed the two little penthouses on the roof? That was where the machine gunners used to watch whenever he was in residence."

It had been the same, the engineer added, with the cathedral, the hospital, the market hall, the schools; all of them had been built by Odria during the last six years—to the greater glory of his native town and its native son. "The moral is," concluded the engineer with that mild cynicism that enters every Peruvian's voice when he talks of politics, "that each town in Peru should provide a president in its turn, and then every place would be as well off as Tarma. But it would take a long time before all of them could be satisfied."

Odria, who came into power through one of Arequipa's military risings and ruled Peru with a rough hand for several years, was a dictator of the traditional Latin-American type, ruling through the army and the semi-military Civil Guard but developing no mass ideology in the fascist manner. His transformation of Tarma expressed the exhibitionist side of his nature, but it was also in that patriarchal tradition that often characterizes rulers in those countries where the political morality sees little wrong in a man of power looking after his own—his own class, his own friends, his own region.

Yet in one respect Odria showed himself wiser than the usual old-fashioned military despot. In the end he felt the current of opinion running strongly against him, and he slipped out of power with a good grace. Just before we reached Peru, he surprised every one by ordering elections that were free in more than name, and his own candidate was defeated, not by a liberal but by a conservative of a less extreme kind who had made a deal with an underground movement that was rich in votes.

When Odria's power came to an end, a wave of extreme relief passed over Peru, and everywhere we met people who were anxious to talk about the days when talking had been unwise; of the dozens with whom we discussed the dictatorship, only two said anything in favour of Odria, and they were foreigners—a Swiss and a Hungarian—who had profited financially from his regime. The stories of corruption that we heard were perhaps the least important; almost no South American government falls from office without such accusations being made, with more or less justification. More damning were the reports of discrimination, and it was surprising how many we, as strangers, heard from the lips of victims. We met young men who had been expelled from universities for trying to organize the students, and public servants pried out of office because men with friends in the government wanted their jobs. And then there were the more sinister tales—tales of the paid army of informers who moved about the towns listening to conversations, of the midnight raids in which journalists were spirited away to the damp penal islands offshore from Callao, of politicians and even generals having to seek safety in flight when they had become too obviously popular. It was all, no doubt, the common routine of Latin-American dictatorship, and the Nazis would doubtless have laughed at such amateur oppression, but the atmosphere of perilous uncertainty that our informants evoked was distressing enough. It was understandable that so many people were joyful to see the end of it all.

But would the next regime be much better? Once again when that question was asked, the cynical look would return to Peruvian faces. It would not be worse, everyone was sure. It might even be a great deal better. But one had to remember that the new president, Prado, was himself a landlord, a mine owner and a millionaire. That was as far as most of them would go. The long years of political corruption, the endless betrayals that are part of normal political life in so many Latin-American countries, had worn away the fabric of confidence until it had become, at best, a frail and tenuous membrane.

As for us, we could form no clear impression. We knew that the political prisoners were being released, that the outlawed parties were being legalized, that the exiles were being called home and the informers had dropped out of sight; these seemed to be positive signs. But there was much that remained of a regime of arbitrary force. Still, under the new government, the spurred and sworded Civil Guards swaggered in large numbers about the mining towns and set up roadblocks throughout the country to examine travellers. Once, in the Cordillera Blanca, we had to present our passports to seven groups of guards within a hundred miles, and on another occasion, in Arequipa, my wife and I were taken from a car in which we were travelling and questioned in a guardhouse by two officers. Where police power is so ubiquitous and so open, it is hard to feel that one is in a country in which freedom has much real meaning, at least to those who are accustomed to rule.

But let us return to that road among the mountains. For it went on a little way beyond Tarma, towards the jungle, and one day we travelled in this direction to find a miraculous shrine of which we had been told. After a while we turned off the highway and drove up a narrow lane, bordered by scarlet wild geraniums, towards a white church in the foothills. It was Indian farming country, and in the little steep fields, where plows would have been useless, the peasants were digging with palas, the strange narrow spades of the Incas. A donkey walked slowly and obstinately before us, disregarding the wild hooting of our driver. The church was very simple; its main architectural peculiarity was that it had been built against a granite cliff, which formed the end wall. A grinning cretin stood in the doorway and waved us into the candlelit interior. On the bare rock above the altar was a painting of Christ covered by a sheet of glass. The legend claimed that one night a group of Indians, lost in a storm, had sheltered against the cliff; next morning, when they gave thanks for being alive, they discovered the painting that had appeared miraculously during the night.

To me the most interesting fact about this shrine was that it had not been exploited in the same way as similar shrines in Spain and Mexico. There was no pretentiousness, no commercial organization. A line of ugly Victorian painted vases, filled with peach blossom, stood on the altar, and three peasant girls prayed before them; the cretin mopped and mowed in the doorway and a car drew up from which two tight-skirted, high-heeled half-breed women from some jungle village came tottering in to make their devotions. That was all; there was not a priest to be seen. And yet the very simplicity of the place was impressive within its setting; it seemed to belong authentically to the same life as the men digging in the steep fields and the long train of llamas that came stepping delicately up the lane, driven by a giggling little girl and following a leader decked out in an eared cap of ribbons and a cord of hanging bells. If La Oroya's social stratifications and Tarma's crystallizations of a dictator's dream of benevolence had their meanings in terms of Peruvian society, so had this little shrine in a remote corner of the Andean countryside. But that meaning had little to do with its overt religious purpose; it seemed rather to suggest the deliberate aloofness of the Andean peasants, still clinging to so much of the Inca and colonial pasts, from all that alien world of foreign industrialists and creole dictators.

Cambodia

1964

EVERY YEAR IN November the peasants of the Cambodian countryside flock into the little Gallicized capital of Phnom Penh for the great national festival, the Feast of the Waters. The event they are celebrating is the climax of the year's cycle, the strange natural drama whose hero is the River Tonle Sap. The Tonle Sap is the principal Cambodian tributary of the Mekong; normally it runs down from the Great Lake of Cambodia towards the main river, but when the snows melt in Central Asia and swell the waters of the Mekong, the channels of its delta are unable to discharge the flow, and the floods press back the waters of the Tonle Sap into the Great Lake. For a season the Tonle Sap becomes a geographical oddity, flowing in reverse; when the monsoons end in November it resumes its normal course towards the Mekong. This is the time of abundance in Cambodia, for now the peasants can let the water out of the paddies and reap the rice crop. At the same time, the Tonle Sap bears down with it a vast population of fish that have bred in the swollen lake and in the flooded jungles around Angkor; all night long the fishermen work with lanterns, and by day their immense catches are dried on racks beside the river to provide food for the lean months of the dry season.

The Feast of the Waters unites modern Cambodia with the ancient Kingdom of the Khmers that built the great temples on Angkor. The modern Cambodians are themselves latter-day Khmers, sharing with the people whose portraits appear on the bas-reliefs of Angkor Thom a cast of features coarser than that of other people in Southeast Asia because of the mingling of an early Melanesian strain with the Mongolian stock. They share also their ancestors' preoccupation with the annual cycle of flood and drought, which is now all the more critical because the great engineering works by which the Khmers conserved the waters of the monsoons have long decayed. The one important thing modern Cambodians do not share with their precursors is architectural and sculptural genius; after the thirteenth century the arts of the Khmers fell into a decline that is now hard to explain, and the Thai invasion that drove them to abandon Angkor in 1432 and move first to Udong and then to Phnom Penh merely gave the coup de grâce to a culture that was already moribund. For five centuries the Khmers have produced nothing worth the name of art; it was left to the Thais, their enemies, to carry on a tradition derived in all its essentials from the Khmer past.

The journey from Phnom Penh to the ruins of Angkor is now relatively simple—a single perspiring hour in a rickety plane whose air conditioning rarely works. One flies over the brown-parched paddies, and then above the reddish muddy waters of the Great Lake, until the green roof of the jungle lies below one; then, all at once, the plane is circling low over the vast glistening square of the moat surrounding Angkor Wat, and the towers of the great temple pierce upward in a pinnacled man-made mountain of purple-red stone silvered by age.

Angkor Wat, the most celebrated of all the Cambodian monuments, is only one of at least a hundred sacred buildings that lie scattered in the deep jungles around Siem Reap, representing more than four centuries of high artistic and architectural activity. Conditions have changed a great deal since the French naturalist Henri Mouhot visited Angkor just over a century ago, in 1863, and brought back to the Western world the first fascinating accounts of dead cities and temples enveloped in the Cambodian rain forests. From the foundation of the Angkor Conservancy in 1907, the work of clearing, maintaining and restoring the monuments has been almost uninterrupted. The jungle has been cleared from the actual temple precincts; the bombax trees, whose vicious pythonlike roots pried roofs and walls apart, have been removed except at one or two sites, like Ta Prohm, which have deliberately been left, for the edification of visitors, in the overgrown and ruined condition in which they were found. Good roads loop through the jungle, and the descendants of the men who built Angkor carry one to the ruins in jolting motorcycle rickshaws; within the outer walls of the temples the earth trails are carefully swept so that there are no leaves under which the poisonous vipers that abound in the region can lie concealed. Now one has to reckon merely with the dense, humid heat and, towards nightfall, the biting mosquitoes that rise from the clogged watercourses that have survived the decay of Khmer engineering.

The Khmer kingdom first began to take shape during the latter part of the sixth century, but it was not until the early ninth century, when King Jayavarman settled near the north shore of the Great Lake, that it became associated with Angkor and its real ascendancy in Southeast Asia commenced. From that time Khmer art emerged as a clearly defined tradition, developing during the successive abandonments and reoccupations of Angkor, until it reached an apogee in the reigns of Suryavarman II, who built Angkor Wat in the early twelfth century, and of Jayavarman VII, who reigned from 1181 into the second decade of the thirteenth century, and built the great city of Angkor Thom, with its beautiful temple of Bayon, as well as other remarkable monuments, such as Preah Khan and Banteay Kdei. Jayavarman was the most active of all the Khmer builders, and the effort he exacted of his people seemed to exhaust their artistic powers, for after his death few temples were built, and those of inferior conception and workmanship.

The Khmer temples were linked intimately with the king's person and with his symbolic role as an intermediary between his people and the forces of the phenomenal and spiritual worlds. Essentially, Khmer culture was an extension of the mediaeval culture of South India, grafted onto an indigenous tribal life and modified by influences from China and Central Asia that percolated through neighbouring Annam. There was no Indian conquest, but the beliefs and iconography of the Brahmins and the forms of Pallava art were transported to the Southeast Asian peninsula by Indian traders and perhaps also by Indian princes in exile. Yet the culture that emerged under the Khmers was no mere colonial imitation of its Indian original. The indigenous social structure, based on clan, remained, and was never modified in the direction of a caste society. The ancient animist cults continued, and were commemorated in the gigantic manyheaded figures of the *nagas,* or serpent gods, which formed the balustrades of the temple causeways. Hinduism became the official cult, as the Brahmins were powerful in the court as they were influential in the courts of Thailand and Cambodia even in the mid-twentieth century. But the Khmers seem to have maintained a tradition of religious tolerance, and very soon Buddhism appeared, first as a popular cult, and then, under Jayavarman VII, himself a devout Mahayanist Buddhist, as an added element in the official religion; since then Mahayana cult, with its expansive redemptorist viewpoint, embraced the gods and demons of the Hindus, there was no difficulty in this marriage of two great Indian creeds on Cambodian soil. It was only later, in the meagre days after the destruction of Khmer power, that the Cambodians turned to the austere Hinayanist Buddhism they now sustain.

Whatever the dominant creed, the king of Angkor enjoyed in life and death a quasi-divine status. When Hinduism was in favour he might consider himself an avatar of Vishnu; when Buddhism was ascendant he might be regarded, like the Dalai Lamas in Tibet in later centuries, as an incarnation of the Bodhisattva Avalokiteshvara, the Compassionate One. Essentially, the king-god was—like similar sacerdotal monarchs in Egypt, Mexico and other countries where the life of the community depended on some cyclic natural event like the coming of rain or the flooding of a river—a combination of the absolute ruler and the fertility god, mediating between his people and the capricious powers of nature. The splendour in which he lived, the grandeur with which he built, enhanced the fortunes of his land as surely as the wide moats around his temples, which served also as transport canals and as important elements in the irrigation systems. When the king died the temple he built would remain sacred to his memory; his successor must construct a new monument to enshrine his own fame and symbolize the passing of spiritual and temporal power into a new body.

Only the sacred monuments of Angkor were built in enduring stone. The king's palaces, where he administered temporal justice, and the homes of his subjects were built of wood or palm leaf. They perished long ago, leaving here and there a carved stone terrace as sole relic, and what we see now of the vanished kingdom of Angkor are mainly the half-filled waterways that ensured its physical life and the temples that placed it under the aegis of divine help.

Of all the hundred temples around Siem Reap, it is to Angkor Wat that almost every visitor hurries on the afternoon after his arrival, and the choice is justified, partly for the practical reason that Angkor Wat, as the only great Khmer temple that faces west, is best seen between four in the afternoon and dusk, and partly because it probably reveals more immediately than any other building the special characteristics of Khmer art.

One rides out from Siem Reap along the straight jungle road, with the metallic chorus of insects dinning in one's ears, until the broad moat of Angkor Wat comes into sight, silvered by the lowering sunlight, with buffaloes wallowing ecstatically near the banks and wild duck feeding among the blossoming lotus. Reflected in it shimmers the high wall of reddish-purple laterite that encloses the temple precinct, and above the wall, among the mopheads of sugar palms, the tall, conical towers rear up, touched with gold by the luminous glow from the afternoon sky.

Already one is in contact with the simple basic elements of the Khmer temple, which consists of a series of concentric rectangles, starting with the moat that represents the world-surrounding ocean, repeated in the outer wall and then in the series of cloistered terraces that enclose and support the central cluster of towers. These towers are the vital core of the monument; together they image the many-peaked Mount Meru, home of the gods, and the highest of them contains, like a dark cave within its heart, the final and secret sanctuary of the temple. All Khmer monuments are built according to regular patterns of this kind. They have none of the bewildering chaos of many Indian temples, and this is because they always retain their pristine forms, without change or addition; each temple was an original construction brought to completion and then dedicated to the memory of its builder in a permanence of shape the hands of man dared not disturb.

The effect of this regularity of design put to the service of Khmer symbolism is a harmonious grandeur that becomes evident as soon as one steps onto the wide-flagged causeway that leads from the west towards the outer gate of Angkor Wat. This, with its triple towers, is a foreshortened replica in miniature of the temple itself. The original stands fully revealed as one passes through the gate to the second causeway.

This is undoubtedly the finest vista in all Angkor. Between its serpent balustrades the wide grey causeway flows almost two hundred yards to the façade of the temple, where the long wings of the first terrace, sweeping out laterally for a hundred yards on either side of the entrance portico, form a wide base above which the inner terraces rise in successive flights, linked on every side by broad, steep stairways. The third terrace serves as foundation for the five towers, of which the central and highest rises to more than two hundred feet, the height of Notre Dame. The effect, massive, yet irresistibly soaring, is precisely that of the mountain peaks that Angkor Wat was meant to represent. "The disposition of masses," remarked Bernard-Philippe Groslier with great perceptiveness, "is so subtle that this temple constructed of superimposed planes leaps upward like a pyramid. The secret of this effect of balance lies in the use of horizontal lines. The upward flight of towers depends on the tiers of extended galleries anchored, as it were, to their base by the cruciform flights of steps which grip the earth with their talons and bear aloft in successive projections on the convex cylinders of their roofs the sprouting diadems of the serrated towers."

It is only after one has climbed to the highest platform and looked down on the stone-and-water microcosm laid out below one in moats and walls and galleries that the limitations of Khmer architecture become evident. It was, in a real sense, a representational type of architecture, in which the viewer was expected to see the holy mountain and its surrounding world in conventionalized form, and in this way Khmer building slowly took on the attributes of sculpture. The recesses of the temple existed for the initiates only, and since there was no indoor congregational worship, the Khmer architects never developed any constructional form more advanced than the corbelled roof. This meant that the temples abound in narrow passages and galleries, in small chambers, but have no large halls like the great *mandapams* of South India. The effect of space is created by opening one side so as to produce a cloisterlike gallery, or by the linear use of extended passages with repeated doorways seen in recessional perspective. The lofty soaring of the towers is evident only from outside; within, one looks upward from the cavelike sanctuary into a conical darkness where the bats flutter and squeak. In the past the most holy statues of the deities stood in these hidden sanctuaries, but the best of them have been taken to the national museum in Phnom Penh, and for the most part only broken and defaced images remain. This poverty of the interior forces one's attention back more than ever to the exterior of the temple, with the rich sculptor's work that covers its vast surfaces.

The Khmers were masters of bas-relief, and the galleries of the first terrace at Angkor Wat contain some twelve thousand square yards of carving, clearly illuminated by the late afternoon sun. The subjects of the great panels are either legendary or sacerdotal, telling the stories of the Hindu epics, the Ramayana and the Mahabharata, or celebrating the greatness of King Suryavarman. In many ways these reliefs resemble Indian mural paintings of mythical subjects; there is the same crowding of the space with hundreds of figures in vigorous action, and the dynamic movements of fighting masses from side to side or diagonally is punctuated by individual combats that cause the eye to pause as they focus the pattern momentarily upon themselves. The carvings were probably made from painted patterns, and almost certainly they were gilded and coloured; even now an extraordinary tonal quality is given by the glossy blackish patina laid on the raised surfaces by the Cambodian habit of running the hand affectionately over the familiar scenes of the great epics.

But as in other Khmer temples, the great sweeping panels of the epic stories are not the only remarkable bas-reliefs of Angkor Wat. Entirely different in spirit, and in the softness of their feminine lines as compared to the hard masculine curves and rigidities of the warring figures of the Ramayana, are the representations of *apsaras,* or divine dancing maidens, which stand out as clear vignettes from the mass of low-cut floral or leafy decoration on the surfaces of pillars and small panels. One type, which appear most often in groups of three, are halted in the cosmic gestures of holy dance, one leg raised and the other resting on the lotus, the fingers of both hands curved back in the classic mudras of Hindu choreography; under the tall, pinnacled crowns their faces smile in mounting ecstasy. These reliefs are broad-based and pentagonal in form. A quite different type of *apsara* figure emphasizes the horizontality of the unmoving feminine body, elongated by the pinnacles of the tall, richly ornamented headdresses; the skirt is no longer swept back in mobile curves by the motion of the dance, but hangs down with almost metallic rigidity from the firmly moulded naked torso; the hands are poised, holding lotus stems at shoulder-height or small round jewels above the navel, and the still faces look gravely into an immeasurable distance.

King Jayavarman, creator of Angkor Thom, ascended the throne at fifty-five and reigned until he was ninety, but a restless vigour characterized his building program, greater than that of whole preceding dynasties, and the introduction of Mahayanist concepts under his influence not merely broadened the iconography of his sculptors and architects but also introduced into the last great period of Khmer art elements that can only be described as romantic. The great bas-reliefs of his most grandiloquent masterpiece—the temple of Bayon—subordinate the themes of the ancient epics to the recording of contemporary history and of the actual life of the people. One is reminded of the genre panels carved by the Indian sculptors of Bharhut in the early days of Buddhist art; there is the same sharp intimacy of observation, the same apparent spontaneity of reaction. Yet one of the recurrent defects of romantic art is also present; the very grandeur of Jayavarman's conceptions and the breadth of his projects led to hasty workmanship and to a dilution of craft standards among the guilds of masons who built his temples under the direction of the master architects.

The enrichment of Khmer iconography through the introduction of Mahayanist Buddhism, along with the increasing tendency of architecture to represent symbols rather than to develop new structural forms, is evident in the earlier monuments of Jayavarman's reign, such as the temple complexes of Banteay Kdei, Ta Prohm and Preah Khan. Approaching the outer gate of Banteay Kdei, one sees through the half-light of the forest the great mask of a smiling face gazing imperturbably from the gate tower; three other faces look out from its sides to the remaining cardinal points, and the tower becomes in fact the sculptured portrait of a four-faced god, representative of many of its kind carved during the last stage of Khmer art. At Preah Khan, as at the outer gates of Angkor Thom, the balustrades of the causeway are no longer the bodies of serpents culminating in the great raised fan of the seven-headed cobra hood; they are now upheld by lines of massive stone giants—on the right the gods and on the left the demons, pulling the snake bodies in the symbolic act of Churning the Sea of Milk to produce the divine essence of *amrita* or abundance. The steps leading to the actual temple entrances are guarded by free-standing and highly stylized lion figures, and on each side of the doorways stand armed guardian demons in rigid postures. In the inner courtyards the bas-reliefs are still to be found, but over many of the doorways sit rows of miniature bodhisattvas, and the syncretism of Jayavarman's religion is shown by the presence in the sanctuaries of seated Buddhas and also of Sivaite lingams. Before many of these images lie withered flowers and burnt-out fragments of joss sticks, proclaiming that they are still objects of worship for the Khmer peasants of today.

Jayavarman's temples owe much of their romantic atmosphere to the conditions under which the modern visitor sees them. Except for Angkor Thom, they are usually deserted. The midday air under the great trees is sullen and breathless, and through the ringing trill of the cicadas the coppersmith bird taps monotonously. The civet smell of a wild animal hangs in a moss-damp chamber, the dried skin of a cobra stirs in the breath of a bird's flight, and the solitude presses on one as the vast pythonlike roots clasp the walls and roofs in their crushing grip.

Time's erosion and the growth of cryptogamous vegetation have also subtly modified the appearance of Jayavarman's buildings. This is particularly the case with Bayon, set in the great area of jungle and ruins within the vast walls of Angkor Thom. Bayon is an even more ambitious monument than Angkor Wat, which it resembles in being a pyramidical construction forming the pedestal for the stone peaks that represent Mount Meru. Jayavarman's desire to commemorate his beliefs reared on the terraces of Bayon more than fifty towers, from which two hundred immense faces—faces perhaps of the Compassionate Bodhisattva—turn towards eternity their bland masks whose smiling lips suggest a secret and boundless knowledge. The mountain image has changed to that of a complex range, and each peak in that range has become identified with the deity that inhabits it.

The tawny sandstone towers of Bayon are veined with silver and viridian lichens, and in the pearly light of the jungle morning the whole structure has the insubstantial beauty of a mythical temple materializing out of light. At this moment the great faces, eroded by five centuries of monsoons and destructive vegetation, do not seem to be disintegrating so much as emerging from the stone in an enigmatic mutability. It needs the hard light of noon to make one forget these atmospheric beauties and see the manifest defects of Bayon. Then one becomes aware of the chaotic planning that gives no view in which the towers are not obstructing each other, which destroys by repetition the effect of the great stone faces, and which achieves none of the masterly balancing of masses that makes Angkor Wat the greatest of the Khmer monuments. At Bayon the failure of design and workmanship alike is already beginning, and the very superabundance of the structure presages a decay that came with surprising rapidity. Most traditions die slowly; that of the Khmers died as soon as Jayavarman departed from the scene. It passed without any long transition from the almost overripe fantasy of Bayon into a nonexistence so complete that even the Cambodians forgot Angkor, and its final revelation to the world had all the romantic excitement of a new discovery.

Letter from the Khyber Pass

1965

THE VALLEY OF Peshawar is one of the great oases of West Pakistan. South of the city the apple gardens stretch for miles along the rich dark banks of the Kabul River, and even in winter the little oranges of the frontier still gleam like gold against the dark green foliage of the groves. The great Kushana emperor, Kanishka, made Peshawar one of his chief cities and there, after his conversion to Buddhism, he built the tallest building in the ancient world, a great pagoda rising seven hundred feet from its stone base to the topmost gilded ring on the iron mast that rose above its wooden roofs. Pilgrims came from as far as China to worship the relics of the Buddha concealed within Kanishka's pagoda and to listen to the hundreds of gilded bells that hung from its eaves. All the pagodas of China and Japan stem from this great structure. It was burned by lightning in the fifth century A.D.

In the pseudogothic museum of Peshawar, one can see the little casket of gilded bronze that Agesilas, the Greek architect of Kanishka's pagoda, made with his own hands to enshrine the Buddha's relics. Around it, rank upon rank, stand the grey statues of Buddha and the Bodhisattvas that have been excavated from the ruins of monasteries in the Swat Valley and the Sulaiman Mountains. Each of them bears the face of Greek Apollo, carved by craftsmen who came over the desert routes from Antioch and Alexandria more than fifteen centuries ago to work for the Buddhist kings of the Northwest Frontier.

All these invaders, Greeks, Kushanas and many others, came into what is now Pakistan by the easy route over the Sulaiman Mountains, the Khyber Pass. The earliest of the strangers from the west was a Greek sea captain named Skylax, in the employ of the great Persian king Darius, who came into Gandhara in the sixth century B.C. and, putting his boats into the Kabul River near Peshawar, carried out the first known exploration down the Indus valley to the Arabian Sea. From Skylax to the departure of the British there was hardly a century in which the sun did not glitter on the spears or bayonets of some alien power guarding the great trade route between India and central Asia.

The Khyber Pass begins ten or eleven miles from Peshawar. One drives out past the green lawns and Moslem cupolas of the university campus. The farms turn into little fortresses, surrounded by high mud walls to protect the cattle from raiders, and the point where the dry shaly foothills of the Sulaiman Mountains rise up from the plain is marked by the turreted fort of Jamrud, which Ranjit Singh, the Sikh king of Lahore, built to keep the Pathans out of Peshawar. At Jamrud there is a barrier across the road, and a little office where the police check one's permit. It is necessary to report back at sunset; the Pakistani authorities do not guarantee a stranger's safety in the pass overnight.

Topographically, the Khyber Pass is a disappointment, particularly if one has come from the Himalayas. For twenty-three miles, from Jamrud to the Afghan border, it winds over easy gradients and its summit, at the bazaar of Landi Kotal, is a mere 1700 feet above Jamrud. The arid crumbling mountains around the pass rarely rise to any great height, and only at a few places does one pass through anything that resembles the dark defiles romantic novelists have described. Yet there is hardly a hundred yards of the road that is not commanded by a rocky height from which Pathan riflemen, in the old days, would fire on troops or exact tribute from passing caravans.

The British fortified one after another of these heights, and now there is not a spur of rock overlooking the pass that does not support at least a turret; often it clings like a swallow's nest to the cliffside, with all the loopholes and windows protected by heavy sheets of iron. Every bridge has its pillbox, and every signal box on the narrow-gauge military railway is a small fort. On larger hilltops stand veritable castles, and these still bear the carved-stone badges of the British and Indian regiments that once manned them.

All these defences were built for two purposes: to prevent invasion by Afghans on the far side of the range and to protect the pass itself from the Pathan tribes. Nobody has really subdued the frontier tribes since Alexander gave them a drubbing 2300 years ago. The British bombed and bribed them but never got them under control. The Pakistanis have concluded an uneasy truce; the Pathans now refrain from making raids, but at the borders of their territory the law of Pakistan ends and the bloodier law of the tribes begins.

Anyone who travels through the pass experiences a feeling of potential violence. There are said to be at least half a million rifles in circulation among the Sulaiman Mountains. Many of them originate from murky little workshops just off the pass where one can see native gunsmiths patiently hand-making exact copies of Enfields. The Pathans carry their weapons openly and, along the road through the pass and in the bazaar at Landi Kotal, one sees them walking with rifles on their shoulders and Afghan daggers at their waists. They move with a quiet dignity that everyone, for obvious reasons, respects.

The Afridi tribesmen in particular set great store on a dignified bearing, and their appearance justifies it; they are tall men with large aquiline noses, fair skins and often green or blue eyes. In conversation their stern, predatory faces sometimes break into smiles of incongruous sweetness. Their costume is serviceable rather than colourful: baggy pantaloons, a long shirtlike garment dyed grey-blue and a cloak of heavy wool, to which they sometimes add a decorative touch by wearing gilded basketwork hats like brimless bowlers and blue silk scarves wound several times around them.

The Pathan tribes are united by their Moslem religion and their Pushtu language, but they are in no other sense a nation. The efforts of the Afghans to embarrass Pakistan by starting a movement for a separate Pathan state have met little enthusiasm for the simple reason that no Afridi sees any reason to unite with the Waziris or Mahsuds who have been his tribal enemies for generations.

No family really trusts the next, and this results in the very remarkable villages one sees in the Khyber Pass. Each village consists of six to a dozen small forts, and each fort houses a joint family. The forts have high mud walls, three or four loopholed firing towers and a single massive wooden gate that is the only means of entry. In the most literal sense the Pathan's home is his castle, and he is extremely sensitive about intrusions into his privacy. Once, my wife asked a driver from Peshawar to stop so that she could photograph one of these villages. He was horrified. "Pathan see you, he go *zing*!" We compromised on taking a snapshot through the window.

In spite of their touchy independence and their ancient cult of honourable violence, the Pathans of the Khyber Pass have made some profitable adjustments to the modern world. While the Waziris to the south still live in thorny isolation and keep even Pakistanis out of their innermost valleys, the Afridis have become the businessmen of the Pathan world. They run the tribal gun factories, they operate the co-operative buses that career madly through the pass, they control trucking services in Peshawar and they operate a modest smuggling enterprise, so that the bazaar of Landi Kotal is a kind of eastern Andorra. One can buy Swiss watches there, tape recorders and even the portable television sets that give prestige in a land where no television station yet operates.

The great past achievement of the people who live around the Khyber Pass was that they never lost their independence; in the classic sense of immunity from government authority, they are still probably the freest people in the modern world. That alone makes them worth meeting with respect. Now they have added the even rarer achievement of making freedom pay.

The Exciting Centre of the Middle East

1966

WE MET JOSEPH beside his cab outside the American University in Beirut touting for Anglo-Saxon customers. He was short, a pronouncedly square man, quite different from the lean, swarthy Arabs who worked on the building lot behind him; he had a clear, fair complexion, and with his sharp, long-looking eyes and his great angled prow of a nose one could imagine him in the bows of a ship of cypress wood, looking out through the Mediterranean mist as the long oars splashed towards Carthage. He looked, in fact, every corpuscle a Phoenician, and the bargaining was sharp and good-humoured. He finally agreed to drive us to all the places worth seeing in the whole of his country for 160 Lebanese pounds, which formidable-sounding sum translated into 55 dollars.

We could see everything that was worthwhile, he claimed, in three long days, from breakfast until sunset, not counting Beirut itself. I rather doubted this, but it turned out that he was right. Lebanon is the ideal country for anyone who—like ourselves—finds himself with a week's hiatus between appointments in Delhi and Rome. It is tiny—130 miles long and a third the area of Vancouver Island. Behind the coast the rough hills rise almost immediately, white bones of limestone showing through dark-green pelt of maquis, and in early March—the month of our visit—a mediaeval tapestry of flowers covers the rough pastures where long-haired goats graze under the olive trees—yellow oxalis, mauve cyclamens and, most abundant of all, splashing the grass with their colour like poppies in a cornfield, the clear red anemones whose blossoming re-enacts each year the blood shed by the dying god Thammuz, whom the Greeks called Adonis.

For Lebanon is the land where the legend of Adonis originated, where Solomon got the wood for his temple, where Alexander and Pompey marched, and where Lady Hester Stanhope, flamboyant niece of the younger Pitt, set up her household among the wild Druses and secretly organized rebellion against the hated Turks. The echoes of the past are resonant in Lebanon, and one hears them most deeply of all in Byblos. Byblos was a centre of the Adonis cult and the god's legendary birthplace; it was also the city whose traders sold Egyptian papyrus to the Greeks, who called the books made from it Biblos, whence we name our Bible.

The cities of Byblos, for there are many of them, lie in layers on a small promontory of twenty-five acres, with a gaunt Crusader's castle on top of the pile. There is an extraordinary brooding atmosphere, a feeling of darkness in sunlight, as one enters over the worn stone of the road through the narrow Phoenician gate. Byblos is said to be the longest occupied urban site in the world. Up on the hill of the promontory, facing the castle, stands an elegant Greco-Roman colonnade of marble, behind it an ancient theatre with the Mediterranean for backdrop, and between them yawn the deep wells of the shaft tombs where the Phoenician kings were laid in massive stone sarcophagi that have now been hauled to the surface and stand solidly under the olive trees. In the lower part of the site, where the grass and the oxalis grow lush in the spring, archaeologists have carefully exposed the relics of successive cultures that go back through the days of the Peoples of the Sea and the Hittites and the Amorites to the first Phoenician town with its mysterious obelisk temple, and beyond that to the chalcolithic and neolithic villages that were built seven thousand years ago when civilization was just stirring into existence in the Middle East.

In Byblos, standing in the outlined foundations of Stone Age houses, one dips into a past as deep as its great well tombs, but in most of Lebanon it is the classical and mediaeval ages that are most evident. At Tripoli the vast castle of the Counts of Toulouse dominates the city from its hilltop. At Sidon only the breakwaters that outline the harbour are left from Phoenician times, and one goes there to see the mediaeval castle that stands on a rock outside the port, its walls half built of broken Roman columns of rose marble, and to walk in the old town that still preserves a Levantine life that has almost vanished in modern, Francophile Beirut; along the narrow streets of Sidon's bazaar the Moslem women still walk veiled and the old men wear fezzes and those curious Turkish breeches with roomy pleated behinds hanging down almost to their knees that one used to see in nineteenth-century engravings of the Levant and had thought long vanished. Even in Tyre the most impressive site is the Roman town.

And Baalbek is, among ruins, the noblest Roman of them all. Vast, megalomaniac, it's a work that for engineering alone daunts one's imagination, so that one does not entirely wonder at the eccentric Russian scientist who a few years ago suggested that the platform of the temple of Jupiter could not have been built by any men living in the ancient world and therefore must have been erected by some long-departed travellers from another planet. Baalbek had been an ancient Semitic sanctuary where Baal, the Master, and Astarte, the mother goddess, were worshipped. When Alexander came and saw the importance of the town as a centre for the desert trade between Palmyra and the sea, he transformed it into the City of the Sun, Heliopolis, and afterwards the Romans arrived with their gods Jupiter and Bacchus and set about constructing their temples on such a megalithic scale that some of the building blocks in the great platform measure sixty feet long by fifteen feet by twelve feet. Of the temple of Jupiter, shaken by earthquakes and turned by the Arabs into a fortress, only fragments remain, but the six great columns that still stand are enough to give an idea of the stupendous scale, and the temple of Bacchus, small only by comparison with its great neighbour, is intact enough to transmit the magnificent theatricality of Roman Baalbek, where scale and setting are everything.

Returning from Baalbek we rode into the precariousness of a present without a Pax Romana. Joseph tuned in the car radio to Damascus, and all the way back to Beirut a deep menacing voice kept calling in Arabic for national unity under the junta that had seized power; the harangue was punctuated by the repetitious playing of "Sambre et Meuse." Joseph's nervy anxiety was typical of the Lebanese during the days of the coup, when little columns of armoured cars and tanks went as inconspicuously as possible out of Beirut towards the Syrian frontier, with the obvious intent of taking precautions without appearing to make hostile gestures.

Lebanon, in fact, combines the kind of luck that often comes to small nations in the modern world with an unenviably vulnerable geographic situation. With the genius for making ends more than meet that they have inherited from the Phoenicians, its people have parlayed unproductivity into prosperity. Lebanon's adverse trade balance is enormous. With little to export from a tiny, meagre-soiled, overcrowded territory, it imports foreign goods without restrictions and foots the bill by acting as the Switzerland of Asia, playing for foreign residents, milking the air routes for tourists, collecting dues on oil pipe lines and generally acting as middleman for the Middle East. Somehow this complicated pattern of services has been built into the kind of economy that gives Lebanon the highest standard of living among the Arab countries, almost complete literacy and good public health services.

But all this complicated act is performed on the thinnest of political tightropes. Internally, Lebanon's national life is dominated by the need to preserve a delicate balance of power between the almost equal numbers of Christians and Moslems. In 1958 that balance was severely shaken and American intervention followed. Even today it is still insecure, largely because the native Moslems are augmented by the turbulent refugees from Palestine who make up 10 per cent of the population. Any disturbance in neighbouring Syria or Jordan is seen with apprehension, particularly by the Lebanese Christians who fear it may have repercussions among the local Moslems. Internationally, Lebanon tries to make the best of both worlds by keeping one foot tentatively in the Western camp and the other gingerly in the Arab League. The Lebanese do not have much use for Nasserite manoeuvres and would prefer to remain on their own rather than enter some great Pan-Arab state. And they are probably the least bitterly hostile of Israel's four neighbours.

Meanwhile, they make the best of what they have. Despite national and international tensions, their daily life seems relaxed in comparison with that in most European countries; it still retains some of the ceremony and hospitality one associates with the traditional Levant. By the end of our three days together Joseph had decided to regard us as more than employers, and as we drove back down the coast from Tripoli on the last evening he began to throw out questions about our plans the following day, and then invited us to dinner in his home. It was all settled. "I have already told my wife to prepare some of our Lebanese dishes."

His little suburban house stood on the edge of an olive grove; it was crowded with heavy French-style furniture and innumerable relatives. Madame Joseph was a gentle woman who spoke little but Arabic and, in traditional manner, served her husband and his guests while politely claiming that she had already eaten. The table was covered with an Asian profusion of dishes. There was *tabouleh,* the delicious Lebanese salad made from pounded wheat, tomatoes, onions and a green herb that is locally called Adonis; there was *kebbeh* and *hummos,* and dishes of chicken and mutton whose names I have forgotten, and the sweetmeats soaked in sugar syrup that one encounters all round the semicircle of the Levant. Joseph's little daughters came to show off their French, taught by nuns from Paris; brothers and nephews wandered in to drain a glass of wine with us and vanished; all through the meal an old Armenian woman chain-smoked and talked in broken Chicago English about the years she had spent in America and the perfidy of the Turks. And Joseph, transformed, was no longer the driver who had shouted "Taxi" at us that first morning outside the American University, but a host as dignified and expansive as his Phoenician ancestors must have been when the Egyptian captains came sailing up the Palestine coast to dock at Tyre and Byblos. "When you come back," he said, looking down his great nose as the evening mellowed towards its end, "when you come back we will drive over the desert to Palmyra. And then there will be no question of money between us. You will come as my guests, my friends!" And, in that moment, he meant it.

A Northern Journal

1969

CHURCHILL
North from Thompson a land that from the air seems infinitely flat. Stunted taiga forest, lakes, yellow-green marshes with clumps of dead grey trees, muddy slow rivers serpentining towards Hudson Bay. For a few miles out of Thompson, dirt roads, sawmills beside the rivers. Then the empty wilderness. Nearer to Churchill curious ice-age formations: perfect circles of trees surrounding piles of whitish limestone rocks, accidental fabrications of ancient glaciers but regular enough to appear the creations of megalithic men. The circles are separated by dull green stretches of tundra. At Churchill, as we drive in from the airport, all the tiny trees, last scouts of the taiga, are one-sided, their seaward branches shaved by the wind of the bay.

The coastline at Churchill. Ice-sculptured Henry Moore rocks, pools white with water crowsfoot, dwarf tart-fruited wild gooseberries hugging the crevices. A botanical frontier; the avens is arctic, but the fireweed is narrow-leaved, the southern species. We stand on the low summit at Cape Merry, looking across the estuary to the stone star of Prince of Wales Fort. The beluga whales are rolling in the heavy currents, their backs dazzlingly white above the cold blue of the water. At evening the Indians hunt them from canoes, with harpoon and rifle. They sell them to the cannery, $1.00 a foot length for whales up to ten feet, $1.25 a foot above that length; the skin will be canned as muktuk, the flesh sold to feed mink.

Churchill—six thousand people spread over five miles and as many subcommunities: an Indian village, an Eskimo village, a Metis slum of shacks—some built of crates and roofed with tent cloth, a ghetto of government officials at Fort Churchill, living in old barracks with utilidors and clubs, all very sahiblike in a northern way, and the townsite itself, near to the docks and the railway.

The townsite: Hudson Square with the HBC, competing supermarket, wooden shed cinema, federal building, and rival Oblate and Anglican missions tucked away in a straggle of side streets, among little wooden houses such as one finds in bypassed and decaying prairie towns; they are worn drab not by time but by eight months of winter. The railway has changed the way of life. Prices in the hotels are little more than in Winnipeg, and the cooking is better. HBC is no longer a fur trade post, but a miniature department store. The highway will be a long time coming up from Thompson—the early seventies at least. But—with five miles of paved road going to nowhere—there are already many taxis, and even a motel. Permafrost makes some other facilities hard to get. A woman taxi driver tells me most houses have honey buckets and galvanized tubs filled by hand. "Perhaps you don't get as many baths as you'd like. But I was brought up on a farm. I'm used to it!"

The gravelly dustiness of Churchill. Off the one paved road, the houses are built beside frost-heaving dirt lanes. No gardens or lawns; even the baseball oval is rough, bare ground, so slow is growth here. Churchillians tell of the southerner who arrived in mid-February with his golf clubs. Point of the story is that he would have been just as outlandish at *any* season, since there will never be anything nearer to a green than a few tufts of mauve-sheened wild barley.

Two ships are standing beneath the grain elevators; one is Swiss! Later, in the Oblates' Eskimo Museum, three of the sailors come in and talk the harsh Schweitzerdeutsch of Basel. It is strange, at a port so far inside Canada, to hear voices from so far inside Europe. On the quay there are Volkswagens; nearest route from German ports to Winnipeg and Regina is via Hudson Bay.

Most of the Eskimos in Churchill are in one way or another connected with the government and relatively well off. But this is really Indian country, as it was when Kelsey and Knight first came, and the Indians and Metis have sure work only for three months in the year, when the ships are being loaded. A few have regular labouring jobs, some fish or hunt beluga in season, a few women work in the hotels, but most are unemployed and on welfare two-thirds of the year. They accept their condition with a mingling of pleasure at not having to work—lacking our puritan ethic—and resentment at their second-class status. They hate the white men as the Eskimos do not—yet.

Polar bears are becoming urbanized. Last year seventy-three were counted in the neighbourhood of Churchill. Ten have been seen at a time at the garbage dump. An Indian was mauled recently.

RANKIN INLET

Rankin Inlet. A long airstrip, stones and gravel, slashing over the tundra. No buildings, but a little crowd waits around the yellow panel wagon of the Department of Transport, the green pickup truck of the Arctic Research and Training Centre, and the HBC tractor and trailer that takes the mail into the settlement. Everyone of consequence is there—the administrator, Neil Faulkner, the HBC manager, Vic Pearson, the Oblate Father Papillon and Bob Williamson, the head of the research centre—

three Englishmen and a Frenchman—typical of the arctic pattern, where Europeans have always fitted in better than native Canadians. We bump into Rankin Inlet over a hummocky dirt road, seated in the HBC trailer among the mail. Ahead of us an Eskimo speeds on a skidoo over the stony, snowless ground.

The landscape. Low rocky hills, bare scanty growth of lichen, dwarf bushes, minuscule flowers. I walk out from the HBC staff house and in ten minutes pick a dozen different arctic plants still blooming in mid-August. On the hillside the great squat cylinders for the oil that keeps Rankin Inlet—this community of five hundred Eskimos, fifty whites—alive during winter and during summer for that matter, since the August temperature is still only in the forties. Above the oil tanks, on the crest of one of the hills, a man-shaped Eskimo cairn: how old no one knows, for the people here are all strangers, gathered from many bands coming together after the great barren-land famines of twenty years ago. Stark and decaying, its corrugated iron rotting with the salt air, the tower of the nickel mine that brought them, now abandoned, still dominates the settlement. Below it gaudy pyramids of red and orange oil drums give Rankin Inlet its only colour. Out in the inlet, the Eskimos, in powered canoes, race around the little vermilion ships of the Department of Transport, and a barge chugs in from Whale Cove down the coast, carrying muktuk for the cannery that a German immigrant operates at Rankin—the only private industrial plant on the whole western shore of Hudson Bay. This year the annual HBC boat has been delayed through running aground elsewhere in the Arctic, and the warehouse in the store echoes with emptiness. This is no longer the catastrophe it would have been in the days before the planes began to fly regularly into the Arctic, but air freight makes goods expensive, and this is a burden particularly on the Eskimo community, since most of the whites are government employees whose stores are brought in by the Department of Transport.

Rankin Inlet is one of the relatively fortunate places in the Arctic. The Eskimos do not like to be idle, and there is plenty of work: in summer construction, in winter the crafts centre; some Eskimos work in the HB store, some in the government office as clerks and interpreters. A few men fish and follow the whale in its season, but though many were caribou hunters (and teenagers remember the life of the camps as part of their childhood), there are only half a dozen men in the settlement who still live off the barren land. They are older men. It is also older men who remember the traditions and, in the crafts centre, stop their work and sing songs for me to record. They are their own songs, personal property, inherited from their fathers. Okoktuk sings the song of the Hungry Camp; Erkuti sings the song of Caching the Meat. At Rankin the drum dance is no longer performed. We must wait for Baker Lake; there we *may* be lucky.

We try to probe for the social structure of Rankin Inlet. Among the whites it is obvious—the ladder of bureaucratic hierarchy, since more than 80 per cent are government employees, with the missionary, the HBC people, Bob Williamson, occupying honorary positions towards the top. About the Eskimos we know only what we are told, which is as much as most of the resident whites know since, like us, all but three speak no Eskimo. There is no tribal structure, since the people never banded together in more than extended family groups (rather like Hindu joint families), but in Rankin, where people from coastal settlements and inland camps came together, an undefined stratification has arisen, with the coast people—more prosperous in the past and more practiced in the white men's ways—forming an upper stratum. Yet some of the celebrated artists, like Tiktak, are men from the barren land who once hunted the caribou.

The Eskimos here have their own community council, their own housing committee that assesses rents for the government-built houses, and here men rise by intelligence and oratory, which is esteemed. But there are other men who, if not exactly powerful, are still feared for reasons older than government-fostered committees. These are the men still reputed to be shamans, who either practised in the past or have received the "gift" by descent. A young woman says there are three of them in Rankin Inlet; she refuses to name them. The white men say they no longer practise. The Eskimos evade answering when we ask this question. A missionary asserts that the Eskimos no longer *believe* in the powers of the shaman but fear him in a precautionary way.

Sadie, sixteen, a girl from Rankin, says of Churchill: "What a big place! Once I got lost there!" One of the men has been to Montreal. "There were four of us, among all those people," he says. "We might have died, and nobody would have known!"

9:45 P.M. The power station hooter. It is curfew time. By order of the Eskimo Community Council, all children under sixteen must now be indoors.

Tiktak the carver. A man with deep-lined, mobile face who seems to be in his fifties but is not sure of his own age. He is partly crippled by a fall, so that, though he does some hunting still, he cannot go far from the settlement. A great humour, so that sometimes one feels it is a life of laughter that has creased his face. A shy giggle and oriental protestations of inadequacy when we praise his work. "I am a bad carver!" He has been carving only five years and maintains that he still works without premeditation, taking the stone and letting the shape that is in it emerge. He wears a singlet, his wife a cotton frock like a prairie pioneer woman, but when he comes out to be photographed, Tiktak puts on gum boots and a loud blue check jacket. A portrait of Trudeau hangs on his wall. He thinks the old life of the barren land was better than the new life. Caribou meat was better than store food, which he and his wife agree is "too sweet." Now, he says, he must work all the time to earn the money to live, because almost all his food is bought.

Caribou is still eaten raw in Rankin; so is polar bear. One bear, whose skin we see drying, was killed a few days ago, and still it is being eaten. Outside the Eskimo houses the flesh of arctic char turns mahogany brown as it dries in the air into food for the sleigh dogs.

A Northern Journal

The Eskimo families all talk of children dead, suggesting high death rates in the past. They never know offhand the exact number of children they have had, but count slowly, turning down a top finger joint for each child. Is this bad memory? Or a lingering difficulty with numbers? Or perhaps some superstitious fear of being too exact? Half the families we meet have children adopted according to Eskimo custom.

Selina, a sophisticated little miss in a miniskirt and openwork stockings who addresses us in English better than any other in the Eskimo village. We find she has been in Ottawa training as a nurse. She is looking forward to returning there. Does she intend to go back and work among her people? She would much prefer to go to Vancouver!

The white fox is the principal source of fur income at Rankin as elsewhere. It runs in a four-year cycle linked to that of the lemmings. This is a low year; Vic Pearson expects to gather no more than $8000 worth to stack in the cool attic above the HB store. During the season only four or five trappers have been out full time, out of five hundred people.

In the south we have always believed Eskimos wilted in heat. In Rankin it is we who wilt, for all the Eskimo houses are extravagantly overheated, to an average temperature of about 75° F.

Eskimos have no vocal way of signalling over long distances, like Swiss yodelling or Tibetan "far-away singing"; they are so tuned to perceiving the slightest movement at a considerable distance that they communicate over great spaces by semaphore of the arms.

Motor toboggans are quickly replacing dog sleighs; the RCMP now search with them, and there are less than half a dozen dog teams in Rankin. Similarly, canoes have replaced the kayak and the umiak, both of which have belonged for years to the museums and to history.

Northern prices. A good meal at the Hudson Hotel in Churchill costs $1.75. At the bunkhouse in Rankin it costs $5.00. An index of the difference between a community served by rail and one served only by air and the annual supply ship.

BAKER LAKE

Leaving Rankin Inlet, we fly over a scape so dotted with small pools that there seems barely more land than water. A jigsaw of blues, buffs and browns—little rock visible—the smooth undulations of the tundra. Suddenly, grey-dun specks fan out beside a lake like a small explosion; a little herd of caribou, smaller than flies, scared by the plane.

Finally, we see the spread of Baker Lake, and the broad waving band of the Thelon River, cutting its silvery course through the tundra to the west. The first view of the settlement: white, red-roofed buildings of missions and stores strung along lakeshore, the lines of Eskimo huts behind them, the buff specks of tents spattered on the tundra beyond.

Wayne Sinclair, HBC manager, meets the plane, with the administrator, and Father Choque in beret and mackinaw. We are to stay with him at the Oblate mission. It is a one-man establishment: tiny church, guest rooms, Father Choque's apartment, all under the same roof. Father Choque does everything, conducting services, keeping the house tidy, cooking, making bread, cutting and hauling ice for water from the lake in winter, helping with the problems of all the people who come to him (and by no means all from his own flock), scanning the shore with his binoculars to identify arriving planes and maintaining communication through short-wave radio with the missions in the rest of the North. He has been here since 1944, longer than any other man, white or Eskimo, in Baker Lake. When he first came, no Eskimos lived here. There were the Anglican and Oblate missions, the HBC and the RCMP, and the Eskimos came only at certain seasons to trade. They lived on the barren land, in little groups of two or three related families, staying put in igloos during the winter. It was only at the beginning of the 1950s that some of them began to stay permanently in Baker Lake. In the past Father Choque would visit the people living on the land. He went in winter, by dog team. In summer they would be on the move, with their skin tents, and hard to find. "Those were good days," he says sadly.

Sound of gulls wailing: large grey and white gulls. The arctic terns hover like kestrels, drop with stonelike rapidity and fly with beautiful sickle-winged grace. Small greyish birds flit over the tundra with undulating flight. This morning a falcon sat for an hour on an old sleigh on the shore. Rarely, white falcons are seen.

I walk beyond the settlement on to the tundra, like a great dry sponge, or, even more, like a landscape of loofah: the tall lichens, pale grey and dull green, matting with alpine heather, blueberry, bearberry and a few ferns; the tiny leaves of the miniature shrubs already turning bright green and orange. In some places purple splashes of arctic fireweed, yellow of arctic poppy and arnica. In the gullies going down to the lake are aged willows, two feet high, gnarled and twisted like bonzai trees.

White men are called *Kabluna,* which means eyebrow. Sometimes this is applied to Eskimos who have become more or less acculturated through government employment. Thus there are three groups in Baker Lake, the few acculturated and usually privileged ones, the equally few (and mostly elderly) ones who try to sustain the old hunting life, and the great intermediate majority adopting much of the white way of life but with little purpose or direction as yet. A people on the way to alienation, but still a generation behind the Indians, and so not so hopeless and potentially explosive; but generations these days pass quickly. At present they accept too easily, with smiling helplessness, what is done for and to them. This is obviously more pleasant for everyone than the resentful sullenness of so many Indians. But is it more healthy? One gets the impression that, in relation to their numbers, the government is doing far more for Eskimos than for the Indians—perhaps trying to assuage our general feeling of guilt for having neglected the Indians—but without much imagination or foresight, because bureaucrats still see Eskimos as *numbers*. The creativity and imaginativeness of the Eskimos are being only slightly utilized, and then often wrongly. Think of much Eskimo art, mechanically produced under dreary working conditions in government craft centres. Think also of the exploitation by official agencies theoretically set up to aid Eskimos. We calculate that, on the average, through the triple markups before his work reaches a store "outside," the Eskimo artist gets 16 per cent to 20 per cent of the price for which one of his sculptures will eventually be sold. A white artist, selling a painting or sculpture through a gallery, gets 66 per cent!

An Eskimo woman, whose husband had received $200 a week before, went to the administrator for welfare. He asked what had happened to the $200. It had been spent on food, soap and paraffin, she said. Surely not all of it! Well, there was also $60 for a bicycle. Her child had been unhappy because his friends had bicycles, so she could do nothing but buy him one. People on the barren land, where tokens were used in trading less than ten years ago, have still very little sense of the value of money, while they retain the old summer attitude of feast or famine (though they seem to have lost the providence that led them to set up caches of meat at the end of the autumn to tide over the winter). Consequence: they buy to the bottom of their pockets without thought of cost or value: imported sliced bread at 75¢ a loaf, small apples and oranges at 45¢ for two fruit. Even at such high air-freight prices, twenty-five cases of apples and oranges vanished in half a day at the local store.

While the whites in Rankin and Baker Lake bake their own bread, the Eskimos prefer bannocks of flour and lard and eat great quantities of pilot biscuits.

August welfare at Baker Lake, $3200. In winter it will average $7000 to $8000 a month, often at the rate of $200 a family. Now—in late summer—there are twenty Eskimo men in Baker Lake earning $400 or $500 on construction. In December, when the work is ended, most of them are expected to go on welfare.

In the Baker Lake area there is now only one family that still obstinately lives on the land, and five or six other families—out of six hundred people—go into camp during summer. It seems as though the last snow house was built last winter, and there will be no more.

Last year at Baker Lake twenty-seven children were born, an astonishing birthrate of forty-five per thousand. One woman in that year had her sixteenth child.

Sunday services in the Arctic. Father Choque rings the mission bell in the morning, and with the single monotonous toll I am taken back fifty years to the village church of my childhood, as in many ways the North returns one to a younger, more pristine age of man. The whites gather in Father Choque's little sitting room, with the geraniums blossoming in the window: the administrator's and school principal's families, some French Canadian and Irish summer workers, the nurse from Hong Kong, wearing a mantilla of black lace. We troop together into the chapel, finding the back filled with Eskimos—but there are some Eskimos also who mingle with the whites in the front rows. Altogether there are less than fifty of us, but the small church is full. Father Choque, in green vestments that contrast with his daily mackinaw and beret, conducts mass in Latin, preaches in Eskimo and English. An elderly Eskimo plays the harmonium, the children alternately cry and sleep, a woman in front of me suckles her child during the sermon. One would have thought this simple but colourful ceremony not as alien to the Eskimo as the Low Anglican service at the other end of the village, but such matters seem to have been determined in the Arctic almost entirely by what church happened to arrive and build up loyalties first. In Baker Lake it is to the Anglican church that the people flock at evening along the insect-ridden lakeshore, and we have difficulty squeezing into the seat at the back of the church, which holds at least two hundred people. Immediately, when I have adjusted my tape recorder and can begin to take notice, I am reminded of the missionary churches of south India, for the women and girls are on one side of the aisle and the men and boys on the other, while the singing, as in the Syrian churches of Kerala, is unaccompanied by the organ. But through the open windows one sees not coconut groves but the tundra, splashed with the purple of arctic willow herb, and the mosquitoes sail in from the hot night in clouds unimaginable in most parts of India. With too obvious appropriateness, the first hymn is "From Greenland's icy mountains to India's coral strand," sung lustily and unhesitatingly, like all the other hymns; the Eskimos are well trained, since there are services on Tuesday and Thursday nights as well, lest Satan find for idle hands some evil. Much of the service is conducted by the old Eskimo catechist, who wears a medallion on a red ribbon over his surplice. The missionary, who came direct from England four years ago with virtually no orientation, preaches in a halting Eskimo, to the accompaniment of much coughing and crying, while the older children play in the aisle with their plastic cars and airplanes and the adults assume a look of seemly and impenetrable boredom. One wonders how much more Christianity really is in the lives of the Eskimo—or most of them at least—than a routine in a life impoverished by the loss of the hunting pattern.

From the mission we can just see the white cross of the cemetery up on the hilltop behind the settlement. On the way there, climbing up from the beach, we pass the one-room plywood boxes that the government first put up as Eskimo houses; the doors are all open to give ventilation. Around them water stinking of sewage stands in deep puddles, where the children play. Beyond this slum of modernization, the tents—widely spaced over the tundra—seem healthier and more appropriate to the Eskimo life; outside them the dogs, large, shaggy and dirty white, lie about at the end of their chains. (Unleashed dogs that wander through the settlement are shot for fear of rabies, endemic among wolves and foxes in the barren land.) Higher up we pick our way between bogs white with cotton grass, sometimes jumping from one spongy tussock to the next. There are berries on the minute blueberry bushes, rather tasteless, and little mauvish mushrooms and puffballs. On higher levels, as we climb, pink bearberry flowers and large-cupped white heather. Also cushions of minuscule pinks. The cemetery lies on a rock platform to which one climbs through defiles between piled cubical rocks, which remind me of some of the Inca ruins near Cuzco. The rocks are bright with green and orange map lichen. Above us now rises the white cross, tall and overbearing. The graves are stones piled over rough wooden boxes, with a small white wooden cross at the head of each, bearing English and Eskimo names of the occupant—Eskimo name in syllabics—and dates of birth and death. Many small stone piles suggest the high child death rate of the recent past. The Roman Catholics and the more numerous Anglicans are separated even in death by a no man's land of bare rock, empty except for two uncrossed graves. The RC's have a stone monument to a Father who drowned when his sleigh went through the ice in the Back River; his body was never found. Anglicans have two stone monuments put up by RCMP for Eskimo special constables. No white men are buried here.

From under the great cross, splendid views of little upland lakes set like turquoises in the undulating land, and Baker Lake itself; its hazy blue waters, golden sandbanks and yellow-green shores reminding one of Titicaca, as the tundra in general reminds one inevitably of the Andean altiplano, one so far up in the North, the other so far up in the clouds, and therefore alike.

Talk with S., an old hunter and trapper who carries sewn on his chest the number by which all Eskimos are recognized—like convicts—by the non-Eskimo-speaking officials who lord over them. He is sixty, and this is his first summer off the land; his legs are letting him down, and there is work to be got with the Department of Transport. Normally he would go in September to kill and cache the caribou that would feed him and his dogs for the winter of trapping. He would take only tea and sugar (curiously Eskimos seem to feel no need for salt); tea and caribou would sustain him through the winter. Often the caribou would be eaten raw, though when willows were available for fuel he would try to cook once a day. If he ran out of tea, he would drink caribou broth instead. Fish he ate only in emergency; even arctic char, which seems to us so much of a delicacy, is regarded by Eskimos as fit only for dogs. S. trapped mainly white fox, with some wolf and wolverine; the best trapper in Baker Lake, he never went short even in the famine years, for he was ready to go far on his own in search of game, relying on his knowledge of the land and a good rifle. He believes in having the best of both old and new worlds, boasts of possessing a dog team and *two* skidoos!

S. does not have much use for the missionaries or for the new administrators, but he thinks there was good in the coming of "the law." Before "the law" came, he says, the Eskimo hunters killed without discrimination, for the excitement, slaying from kayaks with spears and later guns when the caribou crossed the rivers, and keeping pace with the herds by laying their paddles on the backs of the swimming animals. Thus many beasts not needed for food were killed each season. Like most Eskimos and some white old-timers, S. does not accept the view of the wildlife bureaucrats that it was a vast reduction of the herds that actually led to the great famines of the late 1940s and early 1950s. He believes the caribou merely showed their intelligence by not returning to places where their relatives had been killed indiscriminately and by changing their migration routes; he firmly believes vast herds still roam the remoter parts of the barren land. In the same way many Indians long refused to acknowledge the virtual destruction of the buffalo herds. But S. would not like to be compared with the Indians; like most Eskimos, he despises them.

S. does not like the present. He says the young men no longer know how to track or hunt a caribou, and the girls no longer learn to sew; even the Eskimo language, he complains, is declining, since the vocabulary narrows because non-hunters do not know the special terms applying to the hunt and to the hunted animals under special conditions, or even to snow and ice, which have different names in different circumstances. Like other Eskimos, he complains that the present government-controlled educational system, which keeps boys in school all winter and sends them away for two years' residential schooling in Churchill during adolescence, makes it virtually impossible for them to acquire hunting skills through apprenticeship in the

A Northern Journal

barren land. He believes some way should be devised to enable modern knowledge to be imparted without losing the old ways. What, I wonder, would be the opinion of the Beatle-haired young motorcyclists who drive to nowhere every night along the dirt roads of the settlement?

The new school at Baker Lake, modern and as well equipped as a school in the south, but clearly devised and operated on assumption that the educational needs of Eskimo children are *the same* as those of non-Eskimos. There is no hint that one is among a people with their own culture, a distinct way of life. I do not see a single word written in syllabics, or any suggestion that the Eskimo are a people with a great art and a unique tradition. The alphabet is taught by B for Bull and C for Cat in a land of Bears and Caribou. No Eskimo language is taught; even the teaching of syllabics that the missionaries undertook is absent from government schools, probably because, like government officials, the teachers know no Eskimo. Many Eskimo parents, worried by the situation, are teaching syllabics to the children in their homes. Inexperience of many arctic teachers, who often come on their first assignment, in effect spending their time learning rather than teaching.

In the North interest in the outside world becomes less acute and events there seem more remote. There are no daily papers, no television, and radio programs need patience to get regularly. Most people rely on weekly summaries like *Time*, and when the twice-weekly plane fails to bring such reminders, the ever-existing feeling of a tenuous connection with the outside is increased. This is so even in summer, when transients are always passing through. It must be infinitely more so in winter, when the supply of visitors dries up, and the planes sometimes do not come for weeks on end. Even the passing stranger finds himself taken up in the relative isolation of these little communities and curtained by it. It becomes a refreshing holiday from the world where the mass media have so deafeningly filled existence.

Our last night in Baker Lake. At 11:00 P.M. the phone rings in the HBC house. The drum dance is on, the people gathering, and we go along the dark sandy road to the IODE hall—the hall of the Eskimo community. A hundred people are seated around the bare hall. Most are Eskimos; the HBC people are there as well, and some of the French Canadian construction workers, but none of the government people, and the joke goes around the room that the Anglican missionary, who is very down on such things, will have a theme for his sermon next Sunday. Three old women, sitting together on one of the benches, are chanting shrilly as we enter; one is shrivelled to the tininess of a child and the other two are swollen and enormous, but all wear shapeless berets and sealskin kamiks. The drum, about three feet across, lies in the middle of the floor; it is a single hoop of willow branch from the treeline down the Thelon River, on which is stretched a caribou skin, dampened with water to keep it taut. The five dancers, all middle-aged men wearing gum boots, sit together on another side of the hall from the women. After a few minutes one gets up and begins his performance. He holds the drum in his left hand by a short handle and beats the rim—not the skin—with a short stick wrapped round with caribou skin, which gives a sharp resonant thud. He always beats upward, keeping the drum in constant motion and striking alternate edges as they come lowermost. At first he stands, bending his knees to the first slow and tentative beats. Then the speed and the rhythmic vigour of the drumming increase, the women sing more loudly, the man begins to stamp and to utter loud hoarse cries. Suddenly, it is all over, the drum is dropped, the man returns to his place, and we wait until the next man is ready. Even in this dingy hall, some of the magic remains to remind one of the days when this was a dance connected with the hunt; one dancer does a kind of pacing Russian dance, squatting low on his haunches and then advancing on the audience with growls and menacing tread, suggesting the anger of the hunted bear. There is a great deal of clowning, to which the audience responds with delighted laughter; once a young woman gets up and does a parody of the men. When we return to the mission, along the cold starlit track at half past one, Father Choque is still up. As we drink a nightcap, he shakes his head reminiscently. The drum dance, he remarks, will never be what it was in the old days, held in midwinter, in an igloo twenty feet across, with the beating and chanting echoing in the dome until it seems as if the sky would fall.

Lhasa in the Jungle

1970

SOMEWHERE BEYOND the great walls and earthworks of Seringapatna the car did what it had shown every intention of doing for the past hour and broke down in the middle of the Mysore countryside. In Bangalore we had looked doubtfully at the ancient vehicle and its white-bearded driver in his purple velvet Moslem cap, but the young Indian Christian who was to be our guide to the Tibetan refugee settlements in the jungles of Mysore had reassured us. "Young man taking risks. Old man being careful." Careful with reason it was evident, as the car crawled at thirty, twenty-five, twenty, along the road festooned by the ropelike roots of the banyans, past sugarcane fields and jade green paddies where white egrets watched like frozen gestures; through villages where black-greased lingams stood at the crossroads, and once a cross commemorating a long-departed English spinster, garlanded with marigolds and smeared with vermilion to celebrate the destiny that had turned this gentle Victorian lady into a local goddess. Men in loinclothes toiled in the fields; girls in the villages, Dravidian dark, wore brilliant orange and violet saris and little garlands of jasmine and bignonia in their black and oily hair. When the car broke down a little crowd materialized out of what had seemed an empty landscape. Boys cadged for coins; women with lethargic-looking babies stared blankly. After the car was laboriously juggled into operation again, we crawled and gasped over the rolling Mysore hills, crossed the sacred Cauvery and came, within sight of the Ghats, to the edge of the jungle.

At Bylakuppe, the first settlement cleared from the jungle, the Tibetans were not surprised at our accident. They were tough, sturdy mountaineers, almost gigantic beside the short, slight Kanarese of the nearby villages; they dressed in a patched mixture of woollen garments from the cold mountains, and a few women still wore the amulets of silver and turquoise they had brought years ago out of Tibet. Their wide, ruddy faces were burnt mahogany brown from working in the road camps of the Himalayas until—survivors of that rigorous school of exile—they were sent down to join the agricultural resettlement projects that the Indians, with the help of foreign relief agencies (including the Tibetan Refugee Aid Society of Canada), have been establishing to solve in some permanent way the problems of the refugees.

The day we arrived the Tibetans were not working. Nor did they mean to work the next day. It was a time dominated by malevolent demons, and the best thing was to do nothing, not even to pray. Otherwise—they were emphatic about it, standing among bamboo huts of their transit camp, under the tall poles hung with prayer flags—one ran the risk of nine cumulative strokes of ill luck.

I began to believe in those nine strokes of ill luck after we set out late the same afternoon towards Mundgod, the Tibetan settlement to the north that was our real destination. The Indian ex-officers who were running the resettlement project near Bylakuppe with swagger sticks and Sandhurst accents had agreed that the old car and the old driver were useless, and a young Bengali contractor had decided he would like to take a spin with us along the two hundred miles of road that ran beside the Ghats to Mundgod. After slurping some noodles in the noisy Tibetan manner and downing a plate of *momos* (dumplings stuffed with meat), we started out so that we could spend the night at Hassan, the one town along the way.

Twelve miles out of Bylakuppe, a tire went flat. Second stroke. The spare, it turned out, was also flat. Third stroke. We had no pump. Fourth stroke. We had stopped in the middle of a village, far from a gas station. A man ran up with a broken bicycle pump; somehow, he hoped, it would earn him a rupee. There was no other pump in the village or in the cars that went by, until after an hour a little truck pulled up, filled with pilgrims who had bathed in the Cauvery. The driver had a foot pump, and he worked away, holding it down with his bare foot, while a villager held the defective tube onto the nozzle of the tire. It, too, took an interminable time. An idiot danced around us, shouting. An adolescent village beauty in an electric blue sari, with a golden ornament dangling from her nose, stared at us with coquettish eyes; it was Basu, the Bengali, she obviously admired, but the dark glasses of caste prevented him from reciprocating. Herds of Brahmin cows with long elegant horns and great sad eyes, like the cows of the Ajanta murals, came trooping past, driven by men in shapeless togas of grey cotton homespun, from beneath which projected legs as thin and calfless as the staffs they carried. The frogs started up their chorus. The night was coming on.

Standing there in that sultry evening, with the certainty of hard night driving before us (we were to get badly lost before we reached the guest house at Hassan), I thought of the events and the years that had brought us that night to this lost corner of the world. For we were on our way to meet again in Mundgod—another such village—the girl from Oakville, Ontario, with whom we had worked, usually thousands of miles apart, to stir Canadians to the need for help among the tens of thousands of refugees who fled from Tibet in 1959 when the Dalai Lama went into exile; fled from motives they only half understood to a land even poorer than the one they had left.

Judy Pullen of Oakville, now Judy Tethong of Mundgod, wife of a Tibetan, came to India in 1963. But the tale of Canadian aid goes back beyond that to the day in 1961 when my wife and I, in the old British hill station of Mussoorie to the north of Delhi, met a young girl in a mauve Tibetan dress who responded to our interest in Tibetan lore and impulsively declared, "You must see Uncle." Khando's uncle turned out to be the Dalai Lama, and by a mysteriously efficient series of arrangements that he made we found ourselves on a night train bound from Delhi to the railhead at Pathankot, where the trucks leave for Kashmir and a road also branches off to the Kangra and Kulu valleys. Along this road we travelled through foothills dotted with old Rajput castles, through villages where wedding parties were carrying brides in red-veiled palanquins to the clarinetlike music of the shenai, and on to the hill village of Dharamsala, our destination, from whose heights one can see—white tips rising over deodared hillsides—the mountains of Tibet.

Our first meeting with the Dalai Lama finds a better place in my book, *Faces of India,* than in this article. More important, so far as our own lives have been concerned over the past eight years, was the fact that we stayed in the nursery for Tibetan refugee children that Mrs. Tsering Dolma, the Dalai Lama's elder sister, had improvised in a decaying British summer villa on one of the spurs of the mountain. There were four hundred children there, a fraction of the casualties of that great emigration: children whose parents had been killed by the Chinese, had died of privation in the great trek over passes 16,000 and 18,000 feet high, had lost touch with their families.

"At Dharamsala," I said in a report at the time, "the small children were sleeping four or five in a single bunk in the overcrowded dormitories, and many had to sleep on the cement floors, with one blanket to cover five in the chilly December weather at an altitude of more than 6000 feet. The children were inadequately clothed; some were barefooted and few had any changes of garments. Food, again, was at the bare subsistence level, without variety and low in protein; a typical meal—and there were nothing but typical meals—would consist of a watery vegetable soup, doughy rolls of maize flour, and tea without milk or sugar. As a result of this low diet many of the children suffered from sores which covered their bodies and from other deficiency ailments."

We promised to do what we could to help, without any idea

how that promise would come to dominate our lives. Looking back, I realize it was as inevitable as a conversion. The Tibetans have a simpler explanation: they merely assert that a life ago we were two of them. From such reincarnational speculations it is an odd shift to the way our first money was raised, by students at the University of British Columbia, who on the strength of a letter I wrote to a colleague organized a stunt election for the Ugliest Man on the Campus and had the first $370 raised in Canada for the Tibetans ready for us when we got back in the spring of 1962.

I look back, now that the Tibetan Refugee Aid Society has raised a quarter of a million dollars, and has set up children's homes at Mussoorie and schools at Dehra Dun and Palampur and vocational classes at Clement Town and provided warehouses and trucks and teachers' houses at Mundgod, and food and clothing and medicines for thousands of children; and I am astonished to remember that tiny beginning. But the better side of the amateurishness that characterized the society at the start has remained. All the work we have done in raising our income to $70,000 a year, which CIDA will now match in the agricultural resettlement projects in which we shall be involved over the next three years, has been voluntary; we have never employed a professional fund-raiser or even a paid clerk, and our overheads have consistently run at less than 1 per cent. Perhaps that merely shows what resources there are in the goodwill of Canadians if only one sets out to find them, as we have done among hundreds of people who give everything from money and stamps and joe work to design, like Arthur Erickson who made the master plan for a Tibetan Fair in 1963, and paintings, like the forty artists who contributed last April to a Tibetan benefit sale—artists like Jack Shadbolt, Gordon Smith, John Korner, Jack Wise and Toni Onley.

So much for what has been done in Canada—gathering money for other people to use in the actual projects in India. Among the people who put the money to work there were Canadians from the start. Florence Haslam first of all, a missionary doctor whose family for decades have run the Maple Leaf Hospital in the little mountain town of Kangra not far from Dharamsala. When we were looking for someone to make sure our help to the children at Dharamsala was properly organized, Dr. Haslam agreed to be our representative. With a formidable knowledge of the bazaars she bought the cheapest and most nutritious food according to season and installed the local tailors on the verandah of her mission bungalow where, for a dollar and a half in Canadian money, they would clothe each Tibetan child.

Then, in the summer of 1962, the Tibetans set up in Kangra a so-called "transit school" (it was no more, really, than a rough and crowded camp) for the hundreds of children who were coming down in a desperate condition of sickness and malnutrition from Ladakh and Nepal. In this human clearing-house, Judy Pullen began her work for the Tibetans, but she was not the first Canadian there; a figure almost as legendary in his own way had preceded her. He was a student who attended my classes at UBC; a syntaxless innocent of a poet named Sam Perry, who in many of his attitudes anticipated the hippies of mid-decade; he came with Beth, the student nurse who became his wife, and asked me to help them find voluntary work among the Tibetans. They went on their own resources, a kind of private CUSO, and found their way to Kangra, where we were sending emergency funds. It was Sam and Beth who created the first order in the chaos of the transit school at Kangra, scrubbing the children and building latrines with their own hands until they had taught the Tibetans the elements of hygiene, and setting up the first rudimentary classes in all subjects except the Tibetan language, which the lamas taught. After many months they returned to Vancouver, Sam to become a pioneer underground filmmaker, to become a tantric poet and to die in a way that made him a myth on Fourth Avenue.

When Sam and Beth departed, CUSO decided to take a part in helping the Tibetans, and Judy Pullen went to Kangra with Lois James, a nurse from Porcupine, Ontario. There I found them at the end of 1963, deeply shaken by many things, especially their first experiences of Indian methods, but forming a formidable team, living in the same building as the children, eating the same meagre food, nursing and mothering and teaching, Judy rapidly learning Tibetan and devising original techniques of imparting her own knowledge to the children and to a class of lamas she had already organized.

Both girls suffered from the illnesses that were endemic among the Tibetan children: Lois returned to Canada desperately sick and never went back to India. Judy—by some inner process only she herself can explain—had realized that her vocation lay among the Tibetans. At the Dalai Lama's invitation she moved to Dharamsala to train lamas to become teachers, and there she met T. C. Tethong, a young Tibetan nobleman who had given up medical studies in Germany to return and work with the refugees. They were married, and in 1968 Judy accompanied her husband to Mundgod in Mysore, where 5000 Tibetans were being resettled on cleared jungle land. For the Mundgod settlement, the Tibetan Refugee Aid Society had raised $90,000 from Canadian sources, the first major Canadian contribution to Tibetan resettlement as distinct from the basic relief supplies of food and clothing and medicines that had first been needed.

The malevolent demons were still in power when Basu edged the car through the crowds of Kanarese farmers and tribal women and gypsies with big ivory bracelets who crowded the market in the Indian village at Mundgod. Crossing a ravine beyond the village, we climbed on to a ridge and saw the whole Tibetan settlement, a great clearing of brown land stretching under the lowering monsoon sky to the horizons created on each side by the receding jungle. Over this area—about nine square miles—the Tibetans were scattered in settlements of little whitewashed houses, and in temporary camps of grass and bamboo huts. One of the camps on the ridge just before us, with its white prayer banners flapping on the rising wind, looked like the halting place of some Central Asian invasion in this southern jungle. Not a soul was stirring until the inauspicious influences had passed away on the morrow.

We followed the red dirt paths to the hilltop, crowned with a new water tower, where Judy Tethong was waiting at the door

Lhasa in the Jungle

of the new cottage into which she and her husband (he was away in Delhi when we arrived) had recently moved from the rat-infested grass but where they had lived their first months in Mundgod. A little aged physically by sickness and the climate, she seemed nevertheless the same impulsive Ontario girl we had first met at Kangra seven years before; indeed, absence seemed to have preserved a freshness of manner that seven years in the Canadian jungle would certainly have worn away. Surrounded by the orphans she had taken under her personal wing, she seemed well in command of the strange world she had chosen. Somewhat the mem-sahib, as every European is expected by Indians to become, she mingled rather curiously empathy and aloofness; she spoke colloquial Tibetan admirably with the Tibetan peasants among whom she moved, but she did not seem to share the curiosity about the ramifications of Tibetan religion and iconography that nagged at our minds.

Next morning the demons had passed. We awoke to the chunking of the bulldozers working under Swiss foremen on the last edges of the clearings and went out to see the two twelve-ton trucks we had bought with CIDA money going out with great maple leaves painted on their doors to take their part in the clearing work. We walked to the knot of buildings at the centre of the settlement, in almost all of which the Tibetan Refugee Aid Society had played some part: the school which Ottawa Miles for Millions had given us money to equip and the teachers' houses that money was building; the decrepit temporary hospital of bamboo and grass that we had kept going in medical supplies with funds from Vancouver and the new, modern hospital, almost completed with European funds, that we would be maintaining for its first year; the 700-ton grain warehouse completed to roof level, first of two we were building with CIDA help; the orchard of mango trees and the rows of coconut palms planted largely by money raised by a girl in the Quaker community of Argenta, B.C.

At the heart of the settlement, three hundred monks had put down rapid roots; they were survivors of a tuberculosis-ridden camp in Assam, and within a month of arriving at Mundgod they had laid out a geometrically ordered encampment, planted gardens where the vegetables were already high, and built, out of branches dragged from the jungle and mud scooped from the river bed, three large prayer halls gaily painted in Tibetan colours to represent their three original abbeys in Lhasa. They invited us in to make the circumambulation around the walls hung with bright religious scrolls and piled with sacred books bound in yellow and crimson silk and past the altar where bronze images of Buddha and Tara and Tsong Kapa, carefully carried from Lhasa on the backs of monks climbing the high passes, presided over this strange recreation of Tibet in the tropical jungles of the Indian south.

Contrary to the expectations of everyone who watched the first efforts of the Indian government to settle Tibetans in the south (the only region where much land is now available), that transplantation looks like a success. Now, with Mundgod and two other settlements, there are 12,000 Tibetans in Mysore, all under the general supervision of T. C. Tethong, though Mundgod is where most of his and Judy's efforts have been directed. At Mundgod there were long months of appalling difficulty and distress, largely because refugees in poor condition were brought down from the northern mountains before housing had been built. Thousands lived in grass huts while the monsoon rains turned the ground around them into a marsh where sickness bred. Despite the desperate efforts of Judy Tethong and the Tibetan nurses who worked with her, deaths reached the hundreds, until the toughest survived and became acclimatized. But everything now seems to point the path upward. The new hospital went into operation in January. The school is already working with excellent Indian teachers. The grass huts will come to an end in June when the last houses are occupied. The first crops were reaped last season, and settlers who followed instructions did very well. Some of the Tibetans at Bylakuppe, the first settlement we visited, are already self-supporting.

In Mysore, in fact, the Tibetans are making the transition from being relief-fed refugees to becoming members of the mosaic of races and religions and languages and traditions that is Indian society.

Oases in a Fluid Desert

1973

IT WAS CONSIDERED more than a little eccentric in the Gilbert Islands when I kept talking obsessively about the Arctic. After all, the Gilberts do stride the equator. They are the archetypical coral islands, the places one conjured up in boyhood—or at least in my boyhood—reading Ballantyne and RLS. The symbiotic work of billions of minute organisms that grow only in tropical seas built them up by patient architecture from the ocean floor. Their shallow profiles are made tall by vast groves of coconut palms through which the sun filters with such poetic softness that the Gilbertese named one of their own islands Abemama— the Island of Moonlight; it was the island where Stevenson lived during the murderous reign of King Tem Binoka, whose favourite sport was to shoot his subjects out of the tops of palm trees. The temperature never falls below eighty and rarely rises much above. When one describes snow, sitting among the elders in a Gilbertese *maneaba,* the great village meeting hall built of palm logs lashed together with sinnet and roofed with pandanus thatch, they look curious, and then laugh uneasily because they cannot tell you they think you are lying, which among them would be a mortal insult, to be wiped away with the stroke of a knife.

Yet I kept on thinking about the Arctic. Not through the historical associations, the fact that the whalers began the destruction of Gilbertese as well as Eskimo culture, but rather through a sense of the austere marginality of a people who have chosen to live on infertile coral soil and have developed a culture as specialized and as delicate as that of other marginal people, the Eskimo, the Bedouin. And even more, I felt that kinship with the Arctic through a sense of absolute remoteness as intense as I had felt on the treeless tundra beside Baker Lake.

Like the Arctic, the Gilberts are one of the ends of the earth, and up to now not many travellers have been there except on official business. Last year about thirty tourists visited the group, and of those I doubt if more than a dozen got beyond the main island of Tarawa. Tourism is not even encouraged. There are no comfortable cruises or Hawaiianized resorts like those in Fiji, and the one tiny hotel in a million miles of sea, the Otintai on Tarawa, makes a habit of wiring to prospective visitors: "Absolutely no room, Repeat, absolutely." That, we later discovered, was a test by which Peter Barker, the young Australian who runs the hotel, sorted out the enterprising goats from the sheep who like to be guided. Those who want to go badly enough take the chance. We received the routine telegram; we went all the same.

The sense of remoteness builds up relentlessly on the long day it takes to travel to Tarawa from Suva, the nearest point at which urban civilization approaches the Gilberts. That nearest point is 1365 miles away. We left the colonial splendours of the Grand Pacific in Suva at 4:30 on the long drive through Indian villages up the Rewa River to Nausori airport. The front seats of the little Air Pacific plane had been taken out and the space stuffed with mailbags. A flock of white-robed nuns, French and Australian, settled in the seats behind them. A brace of civil servants from Whitehall, in Bermuda shorts, with briefcases and umbrellas, sat on the other side of the gangway from a pair of Gilbertese youths whose catlike Micronesian faces were crowned with chaplets of hibiscus, jasmine and coconut leaves. The smell of the flowers and the twittering of a thousand day-old chicks in the back cabin wafted through the plane. Fat Poly-

Oases in a Fluid Desert

nesian women from the Ellice Islands lurched on board with baskets. It was like being on an airborne country bus. At dawn we flew north over the volcanic hills of Viti Levu, unpeopled and as sharp-edged as crumpled paper, and above the other islands of Fiji, dark and shaggy within their green lagoons.

Then, hour after hour, it was the open sea, dazzling blue, without a ship or an island, a fluid Sahara. The Gilberts and the Ellices, their fellow archipelago to the south, are lost in an ocean so immense that after the Spaniards found them in the sixteenth century, no European sighted them again until 1765, when a British naval captain nicknamed Foulweather Jack, who happened also to be the grandfather of Lord Byron, discovered the island of Nikunau by chance as he was sailing on a short-cut course from South America to Canton. The Gilberts and the Ellices, with a few outlying islands, form one of the last fragments of the British Empire; the colony stretches over two million miles of salt water, but the actual land consists of some 370 square miles, divided among thirty-nine small islands scattered in these fluid distances. They are inhabited by less than 60,000 people.

By ten o'clock the first of these islands came into sight. They were the Ellices, the southernmost group, drop-shaped solid islands (raised atolls) set in the turquoise jewels of their lagoons, and harp-shaped true atolls that are like fences of coral enclosing great stretches of salt water, their eastern reefs built up into series of narrow islands green-pelted with coconut palms and their western reefs mere shoals where the sea broke in white rims beyond which the depths dropped down to indigo. We landed at the atoll of Funafuti, on the ragged grass strip that the Americans made during the last war by ruining the islanders' gardens.

Funafuti is an outpost of empire so classic that it approaches caricature. A coral track goes down to the lagoon through a grove of palms and of pandanus trees growing on high stilted roots. There are no roads in this capital of the Ellices, and there is only one jeep, which the district commissioner keeps for prestige. The district commissioner himself emerges from the modest bungalow called the Residency to join the giggling, flower-crowned Ellice Islanders in welcoming the weekly plane; he is barefooted and wears worn-out khaki shorts, but his accent is pukka. When it is time to fly on to the Gilberts, an old man beats an iron triangle, and we swallow the last of our gin slings in the shack that calls itself a hotel and troop back through the palm grove.

What strikes me at Funafuti, after the lushness and flowery brilliance of Fiji, is the land's utter meagreness; the palms grow out of a grey rubble of dead coral, with only a little green undergrowth. But at least the Ellices are rainy. When we reach the Gilberts, after three hours more of empty ocean, there is no green below the palm trees; the soil from which they rise seems as barren as the sand that grows date palms in the Sahara.

There was room after all in the Otintai Hotel; no traveller who defied one of Peter Barker's famous telegrams has ever been turned away. Once one was there, indeed, Peter and Rose, his dazzling young Gilbertese wife, were perfect hosts, merging quickly into friends, spending hours explaining local customs and beliefs, telling the stories about the *anti*—the still living spirits from the pagan days—that circulate endlessly among the Gilbertese and helping us find means to explore the outer islands. It was a relief also, after the pretentious tourist hotels of Samoa and Fiji, to come to a place where there was no bogus Pacific charm, to a little inn for the odd transient officials and aircrews that squatted in the protective colouring of its own modesty right in the heart of Gilbertese life. The coral road that runs twenty miles over the islets and causeways, from the airport to Government House twenty miles on, passed the door of the hotel. The little stilted houses of the islanders, built under the palm trees that provided the materials to build them, clustered close around it; in the daytime the mats that served for walls in these houses were rolled up and life went on in public view. The girls who lived in them cooked lagoon fish and reef lobsters for us, and cleaned our rooms, and chattered to us in high light voices that turned English into a language of birds.

The rooms, which were already inhabited by honey-coloured gecko lizards that chirped to us in the night, were built right along the edge of the lagoon, and I learnt much in the first days, merely watching and listening. At dawn I would get up to see the white reef herons flapping down to fish in the shallows, and the silhouettes of the islanders going out on trembling catwalks of sticks against the lilac sunrise to their palmleaf outhouses, built over the tide that the Gilbertese regard as the universal scavenger. During the day I watched the outriggered island canoes, their lateen sails spread like great white butterfly wings, skimming with incredible lightness over the lagoon; these canoes are built for speed, of thin planks sewn with coconut fibres, and it is said that an expert sailor can travel as fast as twenty-three knots. At evening, in a long necklace of moving lights, the boats slipped out into the darkness for the night fishing on the reef with spears and Coleman lamps.

Every dawn, and every night at dusk, we would hear, filtering down from the great leaf-tuft of one of the palms before our room, a high-pitched song that had a strangely Arabic lilt; another voice echoed down the beach, and then another farther off, like cocks answering each other in the last hour of darkness. They were the boys cutting the spathes of coconut flowers for toddy; they came scampering down as if the trees were ladders, each with his coconut shells of nectar. Palm toddy is the Gilbertese native drink. Sweet toddy, which is not yet fermented, is one of the main sources of vitamins in the local diet. Sour toddy is a potent and treacherous intoxicant, for alien heads at least.

Fishermen, toddy cutters, children: there were always people in view. They live scattered in their coconut groves, so that there is nothing so dense as a town and even the villages lapse loosely into each other, but occasionally one finds oneself unexpectedly in a crowd, as we did one night at the island's sole amusement place, the outdoor cinema. We entered a great stockade of coconut logs like an old trading fort and planted at the back the chairs we had been warned to take with us. The moon rode behind the shivering palms above the screen; the films were incredibly antique; the newsreel was about the first man in space! My attention wandered and I found myself trying to count the heads of the people sitting below, and failing, and realizing for the first time in human terms what I already knew from books, that population is a major Gilbertese problem.

Yet I still experienced at times that same sense of remoteness as I had felt flying up on the long day from Suva. I would stand by the lagoon. The far islands were a mere furry line of palms on the horizon, and the great stretch of water seemed as much a fluid microcosm, a world caught in its own distances, as the great lakes of the Canadian North. Yet the fragment of land on which I stood was so narrow that I could walk two hundred yards from the hotel and stand on a beach pounded by the ocean, with the nearest other island far out of sight. At such times I would feel out of the world and out of time, as if my past and my future had no real connection with this space-besieged present. I was drifting free.

We sailed among the outer islands on a copra boat called the *Nivanga,* islands with musical names like Maiana and Abemama, Beru and Nikunau and Tabiteuea, and the remoteness was there again as we passed on moonlit nights through the great glistening spaces of sea that exist even within the archipelago. Like the old explorers, one detected with positive delight an almost imperceptible pencil line appearing on the horizon and gradually enlarging into a green wall of palm trees, brown little shacks along a yellow beach, the sea pounding white on the protecting reef.

When we reached one of these islands I would go ashore in one of the lighters that picked up the copra, and I remember particularly Foulweather Jack Byron's island of Nikunau, for there was no reef and we had to plow in on the ocean breakers and leap into the surf, scrambling up the beach before the next gigantic wave. A Catholic priest occasionally, and the district commissioner once or twice a year, were the only Europeans who ever came to this village, and as I walked along the beach a boy trotted up, took me by the elbow and led me into the great shady hall of the maneaba, where the elders were sitting, each against the housepost traditionally dedicated to his clan. I sat cross-legged in the visitor's place on one side of the hall, on a wad of pandanus mats. The elders were smoking pipes stuffed with rank black stick tobacco. The young men were playing cards in the centre of the floor. Outside I could see the women scurrying around, burning coconut husks down to ash in a pit where a pig would be roasted; I had come on the day of a wedding. There was not much to be said, for even the pastor, who was also the schoolmaster, had very little English. But the Gilbertese formalities had to be observed. The green coconut of welcome was presented. After I had sipped it, an elder, his fat brown torso glistening with sweat, stood up in his belted lavalava and made a speech I did not understand. I made a speech nobody understood, and then, with permission asked of my hosts and granted, I was free to wander with a mission-educated youth whom someone had run a mile along the beach to fetch. We went at the head of a procession of children chanting, *"Imatang! Imatang!"* Imatang is the word for white men, and it is no term of disrespect, for the Gilbertese believe that we came from their own ancestral land of Matang, and therefore we are the only race they do not regard as inferior.

The village—its name was Nukumanu—had no European building except the concrete shell of a church they had been constructing for years with the contributions of men who worked away from the island. The rest of the village reflected an economy based almost entirely on the limited range of products the islands provide. These are fish, the coconut palm, the pandanus tree and the babai plant, and the astonishing impression one gained was of the sophistication of the life bound up with the use of these simple things. The babai, for example, is the main starchy food of the Gilberts. It is the big tuber of a plant distantly related to skunk cabbage, and on Nikunau I saw the elaborate way it is cultivated; pits are dug deep in the coral, where the brackish water seeps through, and there the babai is grown in baskets filled with mud. It is—as English agriculturalists have since discovered—the only root vegetable that will grow in this soil and with this kind of water. With equal ingenuity, the coconut palm is used not only for food, but also to build a house from rooftree to ground. The trunks provide the woodwork and are tied together with the fibre from the husks; the midriffs of the leaves form the springy floors, and the leaves are used for thatch and to make mats to serve as moveable walls. The most sophisticated of all the products of man in the Gilberts are the canoes I have already described, and their use is linked with an impressive navigational science that is quite different from ours, based on stars and on the set of the waves around the islands. Old men can navigate a Gilbertese canoe for a hundred miles merely by lying on their backs within the craft, watching the stars above and listening to the subtle changes in the sound of the waves beating against the planks.

At Gilbertese feasts one becomes truly aware of the rich primitive culture that can grow out of a setting as Spartan as that of the coral island. I did not have time to attend the wedding feast on Nikunau, for by the time the pig had been put on the hot ashes in a great searing cloud of smoke, the sacks of copra had been loaded into the lighter for the last trip and I had to wade into the surf and climb on board to go back to the ship. But two days later on the island of Tabiteuea, where we left the *Nivanga* and stayed in one of the villages, there was a feast in the maneaba. The food was no gastronomic adventure: dried fish boiled and served cold, grey hunks of babai like some impossibly heavy suet pudding tasting vaguely of sweet potato, grated coconut and rice, and over everything a sweet treacly concoction from the fruit of the pandanus. But this indigestible meal was the prelude to an extraordinary evening of communal activity. The men, wearing mats tied round their waists with girdles of plaited women's hair, stamped out war dances and historical mimes, like that which represented the coming of the whalers 150 years ago. Dancing clowns mimicked the other dancers and the guests, and one of them performed extraordinary contortions with his stomach muscles. The girls, heads and arms bright with hibiscus blossoms, rendered the extraordinary sitting and swaying dances of the Gilberts in which the elaborate movements of arms and hands convey the intent of the story. After the dancing there was the florid oratory that the Gilbertese love, a speech from every elder standing up before his housepost and a speech from every guest. Finally, one man declared that speech is all very well, but song is the polish of speech, and sang a jaunty ditty for departing guests about a branch that flies away from a tree in the wind but one day returns transformed into a strange and splendid flower.

When we return to the mat on a string bed in the hut where we are staying, after showing our appreciation in the Gilbertese manner by sprinkling the dancers' necks and shoulders with Johnson's Baby Powder, the first cocks are already crowing. This kind of life survives only in the outer islands even of the Gilberts. It is threatened, like the whole future of the colony, by a series of problems, some common with the rest of the world and others peculiar to small countries with little chance of economic differentiation.

Population rises steadily; no Gilbertese feels his virility has been proved with less than six children, and land is becoming so scarce that when a man dies his sons will divide his holding into such small portions that each may get a piece large enough to grow three or four coconut palms. The reefs are being fished too heavily, and the rustic privies over the tide are steadily polluting the lagoons.

Copra, on which the islands depended for cash, is a declining trade, and Canada is partly responsible through the competition of prairie-grown rapeseed and sunflower oils with Pacific coconut oil. There is one island with rich phosphate deposits, which provide work that the islanders share on a rotating pattern so that each family gets a spell of cash-earning; even the phosphate will give out in twenty years. Teams of experts from Whitehall have been working for years on alternative sources of income, but so far nobody has come up with the magic that will make barren coral blossom. The British are anxious to get rid of the islands, but the Gilbertese are one of the few colonial peoples who dread the coming of independence. Alone in the world, they could not possibly survive.

The coral island is a paradise only in legend. One does not live by waiting for food to fall from trees but by hard ingenious work that defeats the meagreness of the environment. The fragile balance of the traditional life of the Gilberts, however, is already destroyed, and now their remoteness is no longer a protection but a threat of isolation that can only be destructive.

While I was there I enjoyed their moody beauty, their pristine flavour, their proud and utterly uncorrupted people; they were too distant, too poor, too lacking even in the basic necessity of fresh water to have been spoilt in the way Fiji and Samoa are being destroyed by commercialized tourism. But since I have left them I think of them with a nostalgia darkened by despair.

Spirit Dance of the Salish People

1976

MIDDEN BAY IS not a name you will find on the maps, but it represents a real place, an Indian village on the frayed eastern coast of Vancouver Island, facing the Gulf of Georgia, in the country of the Salish people. It was not easy to find on the cold and misty December night when we turned off the Island Highway fifty miles or so north of Victoria and followed the winding side road around placid coves and then into a forest where the only landmark we had been given was an Indian cemetery at a crossroads. We found the cemetery—white wooden crosses gleaming suddenly out of a tangle of brown bracken—but turned the wrong way and ended in the cul-de-sac of a sluggish development: roads roughed out, tumbling billboards, a couple of derelict trailers. We retraced our way to the cemetery, took another direction and knew we were on the right road when the hardtop ended and we began to bump over the potholes of a decaying gravel road. We passed Indian houses, slowing to avoid children and pups dashing into the gleam of the headlights, and came down to the water's edge, the black bay sucking at the banks of mingled soil and broken oyster shell that betokened an ancient settlement, the houses lit with bare bulbs, cars parked along the ice-glazed earth road around the beach. Behind the houses loomed a long dark building—no windows but sparks spurting out from the three wide openings in the corrugated iron roof. We nudged our Volkswagen in between the big, battered old cars and the new station wagons, and as we turned off the engine the hard thud of the drums beat in our ears. The spirit dances had begun.

The Salish people of Midden Bay—they speak the Cowichan dialect that Salish south of the border in Washington cannot understand—belong to the southernmost division of the great culture the Pacific Coast Indians created on an abundance of salmon and easily worked cedar trees, which enabled them to build substantial villages and great seagoing canoes and to preserve vast stocks of food for a winter of leisure and artistic creation and ceremonial activity.

The Salish were the least elaborately organized of the six distinct groups that made up the Pacific Coast culture. They were relatively unwarlike and often fell prey to the slave-hunting forays of the Haida from the Queen Charlotte Islands and the Nootka from the west coast of Vancouver Island. They did not carve the great heraldic poles—the so-called "totem poles"—that the Haida and the Tsimshian refined into some of the greatest achievements of artists anywhere in the world. Nor did they develop the elaborately theatrical shows, with complicated transformation masks and other illusionist stage effects, that the Kwakiutl secret societies enacted during the ceremonial months of the winter. Even their potlatches, the great feasts by which Pacific Coast Indian chiefs validated crests and titles by making lavish gifts to the assembled witnesses and even by destroying property, were much less prodigal than those of northern peoples and showed little of the aggressive competitiveness that Ruth Benedict brought out so melodramatically when she described the Kwakiutl in *Patterns of Culture*.

But if the Salish were gentler, less flamboyant and less sophisticated than the tribes to the north of them, their culture did have its distinct characteristics, and in particular a cult of spiritual possession whose rituals were quite distinct from the winter ceremonials of other coast peoples. Spirit possession among the

Spirit Dance of the Salish People

Salish was an individual and even individualist matter. One kind of possession determined most of the key functions of tribal life; a hunter or a canoe maker received his skill from a spirit helper in much the same way as the muse was once thought to possess the poet and direct his skill. But parallel with the kind of possession that determined a man's vocation, there were encounters with spirits who conferred special dancing powers that were regarded as of mainly supernatural significance. Not every person in a band received the powers, and those who did formed a loose kind of society that recruited its members from both men and women who were spontaneously possessed and also from those who were initiated, often somewhat arbitrarily, by the body of existing spirit dancers.

All this, of course, was changed when the white men arrived and the Christian churches went into operation, beginning not long after the foundation of Fort Victoria in the 1840s. The missionaries realized that the traditional societies on the coast, which had no political cohesion, were held together mainly by the ceremonial patterns that validated rank and permeated social organization. The central institution among northern peoples like the Haida, the Tsimshian and the Kwakiutl was the potlatch, whose elaborate patterns of giving and lending tended to dominate economic as well as social life. Among the Salish the important institution was the spirit dance, or "tamananawas," as it appeared in official documents of the Victorian era.

Apart from the fact that their Victorian minds were appalled by the apparent wastefulness of the potlatches—goods given away and destroyed instead of being used for sustenance or sound investment—the missionaries and most of the Indian agents on the coast believed that if only these key institutions of the native culture could be destroyed, the Indians would be quickly converted and assimilated into Canadian society. Accordingly, in 1884, legislation was passed in the federal House of Commons banning both potlatches and spirit dances. The ban was to go into operation in 1885, and the date is significant; it was the same year as the bloodily suppressed rising of the Metis and their Indian allies on the Saskatchewan River, and the minister who pushed the law through was the same old Sir John

A. Macdonald whose tactless handling of the land situation on the prairies goaded the Metis into rebellion.

Insofar as the law against potlatches and spirit dances could be enforced, it contributed, along with the decline in population following the spread of European diseases, to the sense of alienation and hopelessness that seemed to take the heart out of the Indian cultures on the coast during the early decades of the present century, when the ban was most stringently enforced. But there was always resistance and evasion, at first mainly among the older generation who were still devoted to their tribal traditions. In remote inlets on the mainland coast, and in the far villages of the Skeena, the potlatches continued; among the Salish not only were the spirit dances carried on clandestinely but the Indian Shaker Church emerged to combine Christian ceremonial with inspired dancing in a way the law could not attack. The Shakers were founded in Washington State by an Indian prophet named Slocombe who claimed to have died and been resurrected on more than one occasion. Then the faith spread to British Columbia, where its devotees still dance to the clangor of handbells furiously wielded.

Finally, after six decades of agitation and appeals by Indians and sympathetic whites, a new Indian Act was passed in 1951, and the clause prohibiting potlatches and spirit dances was removed. In this furtive way an injustice that had lasted as long as most living Indians could remember was finally rectified. It did not actually mean that the ceremonies started up again (for they had never come to an end), though now nobody risked going to prison for performing them. And it did not mean that potlatches and spirit dances came out into the open. Experience had taught Indians the wisdom of keeping their customs to themselves. Even today, twenty-five years after the ban was lifted, many people who live quite close to Indian villages have no idea that the traditional ceremonials have resumed much of their centrality in the pattern of native life. The woman who kept the lodge where we spent the night traded regularly with women from Midden Bay for their Cowichan sweaters and other craft work, but she was quite unaware that dances went on regularly there —sometimes two or three times a week—throughout the winter. We came to know of them only by chance, and it was by oblique arrangement that we received a barely stated invitation from a chief's wife who was herself an initiate. We were to turn up, and if anyone questioned us we were to mention her name; she would be there, but it was clear that she did not intend to sponsor us in any open way. And it might be a good idea, the message went, if we were to leave our cameras and tape recorders at home.

Thus, by the time Inge and I pulled open the heavy wooden door of the dance house at about eleven o'clock that December night, we knew that the spirit dances had once again become an important part of Salish life. Even so, we were not prepared for the scene that greeted us. The house was made of sheets of plywood nailed on a frame of rough cedar; it was somewhat over two hundred feet long and more than fifty feet wide. Six-tiered bleachers of worn planks ran along two sides and both ends, and these were fairly well occupied. In the long open floor of the house three great fires blazed, six-foot logs piled crisscross in squares to the height of a man so that they became gigantic cubes of flame and embers out of which the smoke and sparks drifted up to the smoke holes and billowed around the house, occasionally half-blinding one. At least another hundred people —men with tambourine-shaped drums in their hands—stood on the trodden earth floor, so that altogether there must have been between eight and nine hundred people there. (We were afterwards told that as winter involvement and attendance increase the hall becomes more crowded, so that by the end of March between 1500 and 2000 people may be present, coming from villages all over southern Vancouver Island and even from the lower Fraser Valley.)

We stood diffidently just inside the doorway, waiting, as seemed appropriate, to be recognized. A man almost as big as the King of Tonga, with a drum in his hand and his face painted black with a mixture of charcoal and grease, came forward, said we were welcome and led us to the bleachers on the right of the house, nearest the door; the chief's wife never made herself known. We climbed to places on the top bench and saw at once that the house was divided between the initiates with their black faces and their attendant family groups on the left-hand side of the room and the noninitiated spectators and witnesses on the other. A few smartly dressed Indians from the United States were sitting next to us in our little strangers' enclave; we were the only white people there.

The drumming had just ceased when we entered, but as soon as we sat down there was a kind of coalescent flowing of the men on the floor towards the initiates' bench. A black-faced girl with a tartan blanket slung over her shoulders began to stand up, assisted by women on each side of her, and all at once, with a spontaneity that I afterwards learned was more apparent than real, the drums began to beat in a distinctive rhythm, and the song—the girl's personal spirit song—emerged (that is the only word that really expresses the process) in a kind of surging chorus, as she started the dance that the spirit had given her, which would take her around the hall and the great fires. She danced with her torso bent forward, gaze fixed on the ground as if in trance, disregarding the spectators, her feet wide apart and moving in measured steps, her hands extended and fingers weaving in patterns that reminded me of the mudras of Asian dancing. In her dance she was followed by a little cluster of attendants, members of the extended family to which she belonged, the women raising their hands upward and addressing strange high-pitched calls to the spectators, as if appealing to us for witness, and as they went handing out silver quarters to the dancers, for every participant in any Pacific Coast Indian ceremony must be rewarded.

As the dancer spun round the third fire at the head of the house, the drums thudded more loudly, people in the bleachers joining in with their own drums and keeping the rhythm until there must have been two hundred drums beating, and the sound reached a thunderous crescendo that seemed to carry the singing on its crest and filled the house with an extraordinary atmosphere of occult power that we felt even on that first dance and more intensely on each occasion as the evening went on. Finally the girl danced back to her place on the bench and sank down on it, wailing loudly. It was the spirit calling from within her, and as she wailed the spirits of the women around her were activated, and they gave strange mewing calls like seagulls.

The drums and the singing had ceased as abruptly as they began, as if some invisible conductor had waved his staff. All suddenly became relaxed, the crowd of drummers dissolved into pairs of men chatting as they strolled over the floor, children clambered over the bleachers, women wandered off into a little room in the corner of the house and came back with paper cups of coffee and pieces of homemade cake as if it were a church social. And then, out of all this casualness, there came another sudden gathering of the drummers, the next black-faced girl rose from her place, a different song surged up, and she made her turn of the room. Five women danced in this way; the drum and song rhythms were similar, and so was the general shape of the dance, yet in each case the hand movements and the stance, like the song, were quite distinctive, expressing each dancer's special spirit helper, and I was reminded of the Samoan women's dance, the *siva*, which is regarded as the supreme expression of any woman's personality.

Inevitably, as all this went on, we were apprehensively assessing the attitude that these hundreds of Indians engaged in their native ceremonies might display towards us, strangers and aliens as we were. Those from south of the border, among whom we sat, were friendly enough, but though they were also Salish they shared neither the dialect nor the dance traditions of the Cowichans, so that they were almost as much outsiders as we were. And we had heard, as one does everywhere in British Columbia these days, of militancy among the native peoples. The lodgekeeper had told us how, only a month before, the people of Midden Bay, incited by "agitators from the States," had closed off all the local roads in pursuit of their land claims. And yet, though we stayed among them until far into the morning, we were aware of no special feelings towards us of any demonstrable kind. Certainly nobody made any gesture of hostility, and later we were in a special way included in the events enacted that evening. For most of the people we seemed to be merely members of the crowd of witnesses, and we were careful to do nothing that might draw us out of the anonymity of such a role.

The men's dances were perhaps more closely traditional than those of the women. The women had worn no distinctive garments and used no ceremonial instruments. But as the dances went on the black-faced male initiates sat shaking rattles, which among the Salish are staffs about three feet long, carved and painted, with crests on their top ends (I noticed the head of a bald eagle and that of a serpent) and halfway down rings of mussel shells that give a thin, dry clatter when they are shaken. When a man's turn came to dance, he would give his rattle to an attendant who plied it as he followed the dancer around the fires. The men also wore embroidered dance leggings and jackets of dark blue serge, from which hung dozens of little bone appendages in the form of miniature paddles. They danced with knees and elbows rigidly angled, performing a percussive stamp and nodding their heads up and down vigorously; the most vigorous were those who wore wigs of human hair that came down over heads and shoulders, almost down to their waists, like great candle snuffers with tufts of feathers at the tops, and completely blinded them so that their attendants had to constantly push them away from the fires. These were initiates possessed of warrior spirits. When the men returned to their seats, they too wailed, but the spirits aroused in the men around them growled like bears.

These were all men and women who had actually gone through initiation and performed their novice dances at some time in the past; they were now validating their status as full-fledged spirit dancers. But all at once, in the middle of the men's dances, an uninitiated girl was spontaneously possessed. She was sitting among one of the families on the dancers' side of the house when she sank wailing into a trance and was immediately lifted and carried over to the spectators' benches, neutral ground. Women clustered around her, speaking to her, stroking her, wailing softly, until a strange, tall figure appeared and knelt before her. He was an old man with the asexual look of those elderly actors who play young women in Kabuki, his grey hair long, plaited around his head, tied with bits of red ribbon. It was too far off to see what this shaman, as he clearly was, actually did, but it appeared to be some kind of communing with the spirit, for he made passes, and then raised his head and twice gave a strange falsetto cry, after which he immediately threw a blanket over the girl's head.

She remained under that blanket for the rest of the night, for a bit of stifling is considered a good thing in such conditions, and when her family left early in the morning she was led out, still completely covered. Her initiation would begin at once, and while she was kept for days in seclusion on a meagre diet her attendants would listen to the spirit speaking through her in cries out of which they would compose the song that henceforward would be hers alone. People who have been conscripted, as it were, into the fellowship of the dancers often have to go through severe hazings, but those who are spontaneously possessed are treated with special gentleness.

Now began the part of the ceremonial without which none of the dances we had seen would be regarded as valid; the only way of validation is through giving on the part of the initiates' families. Men and boys began to come into the house carrying cardboard cartons that were piled in a long row in front of the initiates' benches. Then, one by one, the family groups began their round of the bleachers, the black-faced dancer making the gifts, and an elder in each group, expert at rank, pointing out each recipient.

Blankets were—in keeping with tradition—the principal gifts, and a person's status was made publicly evident by the kind of blanket he received. High rank (which usually means you have made rich gifts in the past) merited five-point Hudson's Bay blankets; low rank (which means meagre giving in the past) merited only hideously flowered flannelette sheets. We ranked neither blankets nor the silk scarves with the rhinestone jewels knotted in the corners that formed the second round of gifts. Still, we were witnesses, our presence helped to validate the dances, and we were rewarded during the later rounds, when crockery and fruit were given out; we had to accept, for refusal of a gift would have publicly shamed the dancer and his whole clan. Gift after gift was sent up, hand over hand, to our place at the top of the bleachers; when we counted them afterwards we found that we had collected one gold-and-white cup and saucer, one large rose-patterned ironstone plate, one glass mug, one Pyrex dish, four oranges and fourteen apples. Such gifts indicated that our presence and our behaviour had been accepted. They also gave some means of judging the quantity of goods changing hands that night, for we were only minor recipients among the three or four hundred people who sat on the spectators' benches. One gigantic woman sitting just below us went out with three large cardboard cartons filled with her presents, and the combined families must have spent several thousand dollars in such gifts alone.

Nor were these the only transfers of property, for every occasion like this is used as an opportunity for the public settling of ceremonial debts, and the floor was taken up for at least an hour, while the families went round with their gifts, by men making orations in ceremonial Salish as various obligations were straightened out by the handing over of prominently displayed bundles of bills, whose amount was always declared on spread fingers raised high for everyone to see. Several hundred dollars changed hands in this way in addition to the gifts made to the witnesses on the right-hand benches.

It was after the giving that two isolated dances took place, and these in their different ways were the most moving episodes of the night. A small boy led in a young man in a strange garb of jerkin and leggings of grey and white wool, with many tassels, and a headdress coming down over the face, rather like that of the warrior dancers except that it also was made of much-tasselled grey and white wool. He carried a tasselled spear on whose point someone had stuck a big, red apple.

He was a novice dancer in a state of possession, and according to Salish beliefs a highly dangerous figure who had to be watched carefully lest he go berserk and start attacking people with his spear. This young man, however, did nothing but wander vaguely around the floor until the drums began to beat; this threw him into his dancing frenzy, and he covered the circuit of the house twice in a series of extraordinary sightless leaps, bouncing up and down with his knees and feet tightly together, as if he were made of rubber, and giving a great deal of trouble to the small attendant who had to keep him from jumping into one of the fires. At last he sank down on a bench at the far end of the house, well away from the actual initiates, and there the spirit wailed in him like a wolf for a good hour before he finally settled into a silent trance. Nobody took any notice of all this. It was obviously what a respectable, traditionally minded young man was expected to do in Salish society.

This performance of a young man beginning his career of spiritual possession was balanced by the other late dance, which clearly marked an end. An ancient woman had been sitting in the middle of the dancers' bench, and now she was being helped to her feet by her daughters and granddaughters. She was almost skeletally fragile and dressed in a pink sequinned gown and a rhinestoned headband with a few white eagle feathers stuck in it; her cheeks seemed to have been dusted with wood ash, for they had an unnatural greyness. She was so weak that she had to be supported in her slow walk, and all that remained of her dance was the continual movement of her hands and fingers in the gestures that expressed her spirit. Yet it was in one way the most dramatic dance of the whole night, for the drummers came out of the bleachers to join those on the floor and make an avenue of sound through which the old dancer progressed, with hundreds of voices shouting out her song, and her attendants scattering handfuls of coins among the drummers and singers. It was obviously a farewell, for we felt no doubt that this was the old woman's last dance, and that she and everyone else knew it. But it was also a kind of assertion of continuity, for here was a person who had been a child in the last flourishing of the old native culture, and by supporting her in her dance the rest of the people were not only proclaiming their continuity with that past but were also celebrating the revival of the old ways.

Somewhere past three in the morning the crowds on the bleachers began to thin as people set out on the way home to other villages, and we went out with them. We were elated by what we had seen, above all by what we had heard and felt in the vast vibrations of sound that surged about the great house. On Inge, indeed, the effect had been more than elation. For weeks she had been suffering from arthritis, leading to a pinched nerve that caused agonizing headaches, and only her intense interest in native life had led her to take the risk of sitting all night in a draughty longhouse with the temperature outside hovering near freezing point. But the expected surges of pain never came, and as she went out she felt completely cured. For ten days afterwards she was entirely free of pain, and her physiotherapist, who himself was experimenting with ultrasonic vibrations, was not surprised; he believed it had been due to the sustained vibrations of so many drums over several hours. Certainly Inge's experience bore out what we had been told before we went to Midden Bay: that initiation into the spirit dances cures a wide variety of sicknesses that are in some way or another psychosomatic.

But it seemed to us not merely a matter of individual cure but of the cure of a whole people from the alienation of those intermediate generations when they had lived between two worlds, their native culture almost completely destroyed and the culture of the white man temperamentally alien to them. It seemed as though time had taken a spiral, and now they were in possession again of the heart of their culture, the spirit dance cult, which expressed their collective Salish identity and at the same time emotionally supported each individual as the old communal Indian life had done. Quite apart from the sense of occult power produced by the drumming and singing, one recognized a feeling of confidence and pride among the hundreds of people gathered in the dance house. Here they were in their own world, secure, and that was perhaps why they could accept the two of us without either the shy embarrassment or the nervous hostility that so often spoils relations between Indians and whites. It was a sign of the reverence with which the people of Midden Bay regard their revived pagan ceremonies that—despite cynical forewarnings by local whites—we saw no one in the great house who was either drinking or even mildly drunk, and when we went outside there was none of the drinking in cars that accompanies white dances in Vancouver Island village halls.

Next morning we went down again to Midden Bay to see in the daylight what the village looked like. It was little different from other Vancouver Island Indian villages. The cemetery at the crossroads was a rough field where gaudy, plastic flowers were the only decorations. The houses were ill-maintained, the gardens grew only rubbish, and if it had not been for some expensive station wagons and pickup trucks, one would have thought Midden Bay one of the poorest places in Canada. This was not really so, for the Indians here were relatively prosperous, many of the men earning well from fishing and most of the others having regular work in the local sawmills. It was merely that they had different ideas on how money was well spent; that night of ceremony and giving convinced me that they were right.

From Rotorua to Tasman Bay

1979

YOU TRAVEL MOST of the Pacific from Los Angeles in darkness. Dawn brightens over a glittering sea that continues for another thousand miles without rocks or islands: the vast empty sea over which Polynesians voyaged from Samoa in their great canoes six centuries ago to found the Maori settlements of New Zealand. They called it Aotearoa, the Long Bright Land.

Most of the passengers on our flight were Australians going on to Sydney. But the woman beside me was a New Zealander, and as we approached her country, she began to talk about returning home. Twenty years ago she had gone into the world for a life New Zealand seemed too narrow to provide. She told how she had worked in England, Hong Kong, Malta, Canada, and at times she spoke with zest and gratitude. Then the shadow came over her face, shutting out the youth, bringing on the middle age.

"Now I'm going back. The rest of the world is killing itself."

"Do you think home will be any better?" I asked.

She gave an odd, grim look, as if I expressed her own doubt. "I don't think we've gone so far," she said slowly. "We're not so polluted. We don't hate each other so much. We're a minor, backward country without a history. I never thought I'd thank God for that. But I do."

She stirred in my mind that old novelist's vision—Samuel Butler's and Aldous Huxley's—of New Zealand as the far corner of a ruined world where a germ of civilization might survive to fecundate a second spring of humanity. A land with an undefined future; a land without a history.

New Zealand slid into sight beneath us in a scatter of islands, their western shores white with surf. Descending over pastures bright as bowling greens, where the cattle fed in great black-and-white Holstein herds undisturbed by the plane's noise, we landed at Auckland's airport.

Auckland is one of those cities—like Hong Kong and Vancouver—where land and sea interlock to create magnificent natural settings. Here the long upper arm of the North Island is almost severed by inlets that bite deeply into the land. The plain between the inlets has volcanic soil so rich that when the whalers and missionaries arrived it was the most densely populated part of Aotearoa. When traders introduced firearms, the local warriors massacred each other so efficiently that by 1840 Captain Hobson was able to found there the first capital of the British colony of New Zealand.

Auckland's special scenic feature is a score of small extinct volcanoes from whose summits one looks out over the glittering harbours. Manukau to the west was formerly a sailing-ship haven; now, too shallow for modern ships, it is inhabited by the 40,000 sailing dinghies and yachts (one for every twenty Aucklanders) that at weekends crowd the waters like flocks of floating butterflies. Waitemata is the modern port where the cruise ships and freighters dock and to which the city is oriented.

The view from Auckland's little volcanoes shows how sadly the setting has been misused. Except for a tight centre dominated by the Gothic hilltop towers of the university, Auckland is a vast anti-greenbelt to which at night the workers depart, leaving the centre to tourists and night watchmen. New Zealanders believe fanatically that every man's home is his castle, and their cities (Auckland is the largest with 800,000 people,

Wellington next with 350,000) are afflicted not with high-rise apartments shutting out the sun but with sprawling, red-tin-roofed bungalow suburbs through which one drives for miles of sameness to reach the pastoral countryside on which New Zealand depends for its life.

Even in Auckland's centre there was little that was impressive except for the great parks full of enormous old trees that exist in all New Zealand cities. Victorian warehouses built with round grave arches and massive buttresses to withstand earthquakes had an impassive Roman kind of dignity; a few old hotels were given adventitious charm by silver-painted traceries of fire escapes clambering with apparent caprice over their façades; glass-roofed Edwardian arcades harboured boutiques and teashops frequented by old ladies of improbable ornateness and fragility. Such things aroused only nostalgia. They reminded me of childhood in time-halted corners of England rather than evoking a characteristically New Zealand past to which one might give the name of history.

A century ago Anthony Trollope (still popular in the Antipodes) sensed this relationship of New Zealand to the distant homeland. Of the New Zealander he said: "He admits the supremacy of England to every place in the world, only he is more English than any Englishman at home. He tells you he has the same climate, only somewhat improved; that he grows the same produce, only with somewhat heavier crops; that he has the same beautiful scenery at his doors, only somewhat grander in its nature and more diversified in its details; that he follows the same pursuits and after the same fashion, but with less of misery, less of want, and a more general participation in the gifts which God has given to the country."

What Trollope said is still largely true. From the start, New Zealand's immigration policy made it more British than any other dominion. Here were no equivalents of the Québécois or the Afrikaners or even the Italians after the Second World War in Australia. The pattern was set with early migrations sponsored by philanthropists like Edward Gibbon Wakefield, whose colonists founded Wellington in 1840, or by religious bodies like the Free Church of Scotland, which founded granite

Dunedin in 1848, or the Church of England, whose followers founded Christchurch in 1850 and gave it a cathedral designed by the great Gothic revivalist Giles Gilbert Scott. A tenth of New Zealanders are Polynesians—Maoris or immigrants from Samoa and the Cook Islands. The rest are still almost wholly British by descent, and London is their cultural mecca. New Zealanders see mainly BBC television programs.

In some ways the influence was good. An imported vein of Victorian radicalism led to pioneer innovations: votes for women in 1893, old-age pensions in 1898. Since then it has congealed into a rather stifling welfare paternalism, one of whose results is something worse than the traditional English Sunday; in New Zealand shops close from Friday night to Monday morning, and most restaurants put up the shutters on Sunday. Not long ago pubs closed at 6:00 P.M., and the habit of drinking against time survives. Enter an Auckland bar any time between five and eight and you risk being drawn into a fast-drinking circle of total strangers and treated to great glasses of strong New Zealand beer with a good fellowship from which you must escape quickly if you are to escape upright.

New Zealand beer more than lives up to English traditions. Local wines have improved greatly and are better than Canadian. But a meal is still a gamble, the dice loaded against the eater. The rule I learned was that plain cooking in New Zealand is usually good. You are rarely let down by lamb with mint sauce, or steak-and-kidney pie, or trifle. Local fish like tarakihi, trevally and hapuku are often excellent, as are mussels and oysters. But any kind of elaborate cooking usually means good food spoiled. We learned, when we reached a hotel that prided itself on a gourmet kitchen, to head into the back streets, or the nearest village if it was in the country, and seek out some modest shack that featured steak and chicken dinners without frills.

Little history, and a cultural colonialism more rampant than Peggy Atwood ever dreamed of; dull cities and dead weekends; New Zealand is no place for self-respecting culture vultures to alight. But that accentuates the good things that await a patient traveller. After the first few days one either seeks the next plane out or confronts the country and its people directly, with no myths intervening. Fortunately, country and people are both eminently accessible, and the hinterland has more to offer than the cities seem to promise. It is as a land, in a physical and literal sense, rather than as a nation, which it hardly is, that New Zealand is worth seeing.

Since New Zealand is not really a country of destinations, where one leaps from one centre of life and culture to the next, it has to be experienced while you travel, and the most rewarding way to travel is by bus. The Road Services of the New Zealand Railways crisscross most of the country; where they are absent there are regular private services. All these buses work on mail runs, which means that towns and settlements on the way are visited, with frequent stops at the ubiquitous New Zealand tearooms to eat scones, pikelets, sausage rolls, meat pies filled with strange brown glue, and a vast array of cakes and sandwiches; New Zealanders have an enviable ability to consume vast quantities of starchy foods and still retain reasonably trim figures. Often the coaches stop at ranches to pick up mail bags and at remote houses to toss out newspapers; one feels involved in the life of the country. The routes reach Cape Reinga at the farthest tip of the North Island (where the bus runs over the sands of the vast Ninety Mile Beach) and a thousand miles south to Invercargill on South Island, where even in January (the New Zealand high summer) snows may blow up from the frozen southern polar regions. They also traverse the mountain passes on both islands, so that in three or four weeks you can see all the varieties of New Zealand scenery at no great cost, and in the process get a good feel of the way of living in the one agrarian country that lives on the level of the western industrial nations.

My choice of travel from Auckland starts by defying New Zealand recommendations, which always begin by suggesting a start at the Bay of Islands 180 miles or so north of the city. This is a predilection born of the beach summers of Auckland childhoods. In fact, the scenery of this complex of inlets and low islets is insipid, and there is nothing to do except fish tunny and marlin. Instead, it is best to start south at once, heading into the pastoral Waikato region and on to the Maori heartland of Rotorua.

On this road, passing through places with sonorous Maori names like Otahuhu and Papakirua, we got a first sight of what primeval New Zealand looked like to the explorers. Copses of bright green mangrove reached out on stilted roots over estuary mud flats; among them strutted strange waders called pukekos like giant coots with blue breasts and red beaks. In the deep gullies wild bush survived, looking like old engravings of Amazonian jungle; tall, umbrella-topped trees, covered with swordleafed epiphytes, hung with lianas; an undergrowth of fortyfoot tree ferns and ragged pandanuses. The rain forests of South Island show New Zealand jungle far more abundantly, but these North Island fragments suggest how wild and impenetrable the land must have seemed before the settlers felled and burned and made it one of the most grazed and cultivated countries in the world, with a dairy industry that maintains three cows for every human New Zealander.

One lush pasture monotonously followed another, filled with fat cows, dotted with wooden farmhouses shaded by magnolias, and offering here and there some mild surprise like an English hedgehog scurrying over the road. The hedgehog's ancestors were imported by the first settlers, who wanted to recreate in detail England's green and pleasant land, and who also introduced the rabbit, which ate up the pastures. To deal with rabbits, they imported stoats, but the stoats killed native groundbreeding songbirds, and English blackbirds were brought to replace them. A classic example of how an easily adaptable foreign species can destroy an ancient ecosystem. Today even the New Zealander's totem bird, the shy nocturnal kiwi, may be nearing extinction.

Yet one curious native species was spectacularly present on the way to Rotorua. At the edge of the North Island's central massif of limestone cliffs and volcanic crags a wooded gorge led to the Waitomo caves. They were limestone caves with stalactites, narrow passages that stirred my claustrophobia, vaulted chambers that relieved it, dark underground rivers. What made them different were the so-called "glowworms," larvae of an ephemeral water fly, *Arachnocampo luminosa*. A gigantic Maori Charon took us on the underground river in a leaky scow that he propelled by pushing on spurs of rock that came perilously near our heads as we drifted into the darkness of the inner caves. We had been told to be silent, for noise makes the glowworms switch off, and the quietness, broken by the soft swishing of the river, intensified the inrush of pure wonder as we entered the chamber lit by dense galaxies of turquoise points of light, shining steadily against the dark night of the rock like an elfin miniature of heaven and reflected in the dark water beneath. It was a bizarre, haunting sight, a hidden sunless world of abstract beauty.

You descend from the hills into Rotorua through wastes of volcanic ash and rough maquis, until the wide grey lake appears, with the Victorian resort town beside it, and the hot springs fill the air with a stench like a badly run pulp mill. Maoris are numerous in Rotorua; they own much of the land and control much of the tourist trade. Our night's entertainment was a show of Maori clowning and dancing, mostly to lilting tunes borrowed from hot-Gospelling missionaries. On a headland steamy with vapours from the springs, we found a Maori village with a big, ornately carved and vermilion-painted meeting house; an old man quietly whittled wooden images for sale, and little girls in front of a lava-rock statue of Queen Victoria offered in precise mission English to sing a Maori song; they screeched a hymn. Another clan of Maoris lived by organizing tours through the weird Whakarewarewa Valley. On the scrubby hillsides, where a chill trout stream ran between farting pools of boiling mud and geysers steamed up fifty feet into the air, they had built some creditable reconstructions of traditional forts, and we felt nearer to a real past here than anywhere else in New Zealand.

You can get the best out of the North Island by going from Rotorua to Lake Taupo in the mountains and then through the river gorges to the west coast at New Plymouth, a fretwork Victorian town settled by Devon men in 1841. The isolated 2500-metre cone of Mount Egmont towers over New Plymouth, looking so much like Fujiyama that it draws a regular traffic of Japanese. We followed the coast south to the capital, windy Wellington, where the gusts blow at more than thirty knots for an average of 188 days a year. The National Museum has the best collection I know of Cook-period Maori artifacts, and the new parliament building, designed by Sir Basil Spence and looking like a gargantuan egg with the bottom cut off (New Zealanders call it the Beehive) is worth a glance. Not much else justifies braving Wellington gusts and gales, and we soon crossed Cook Strait by the car ferry, which sails through the rugged-shored Marlborough inlets to Picton, where we took the bus down the east-coast road, with its broad empty beaches and bold headlands, to Christchurch.

The landscaped banks of the Avon River form an attractive serpentine park meandering through the heart of Christchurch, which is the best base for journeys in the South Island. Mount Cook, almost 3300 metres high and the country's tallest mountain, was obviously our first destination. We went southwest over the Canterbury wheatlands and up the gorge of the Waitaki River into the dry grasslands, whose tussocked pastures support most of the 70 million New Zealand sheep. The sheep are scattered over a vast area of hill country with meagre grazing; only when we saw hillsides white with flocks rounded up for shearing did we have a physical sense of what such numbers mean.

Mount Cook dominates the Southern Alps that fence off the sheep country to the west; it rises 12,000 awesome feet sheer from a lowish valley at the head of Lake Pukaki. I have seen much higher mountains in the Andes, the Rockies, the Himalayas, but have never felt so close to natural vastness, and the grand pyramid of Cook stays in my memory as the most satisfying mountain I know to stare at, lounging in a meadow and eating wild gooseberries at its foot, willing to contemplate, never hoping to conquer.

The other natural sights not to be missed on the South Island are the deep fjords on the southwestern coast and the glaciers to the north. The grandest fjord is Milford Sound. We reached it by a devious journey through the old Otago gold fields and then over the passes into the west-coast rain forest, whose dense evergreen cover, flowing down to dip its branches in salt water, gives the tight trench of Milford Sound a special quality of menacing luxuriance. Even as a Vancouverite remembering Howe Sound, I was impressed, particularly as we had struck one of the sound's few fine days; the rainfall averages somewhat over eight metres a year.

Another coil of mountain roads, another pass looping down into the rain forests, brought us to the Fox and Franz Josef glaciers, which dip wondrously near to the sea. Not even a small climb is necessary to see them. At Franz Josef the road emerges out of a tree-fern jungle at 500 feet, and there the blue-glittering pinnacles confront one, with the main glacier opening upward, a vast glittering fan of ice tipped by the jagged peaks of Mount Tasman. We stood admiring, and a flock of keas, olive-green mountain parrots with bright vermilion underwings, came swooping out of the forest; the driver hurried to defend his bus as they began to tear the rubber of the windshield wipers with tough curved beaks.

The gentle orchard lands of Nelson, the fine coastline of Tasman Bay where the Dutch were driven off by Maoris in 1642; I could continue indefinitely on the lesser sights of the South Island. It all comes back to the fact that what one sees and finds in New Zealand is the land itself. As for New Zealand society, let me confess at the end a haunting sense of déjà vu. What I remembered was the nineteenth-century anglophone society of the Canadian west coast that I found surviving in Victoria when I got there thirty years ago. I could not help thinking, as I looked at New Zealand with that memory in mind, how narrowly Canadians had escaped a continuing colonialism. "There," I thought, "but for the grace of Quebec, go we!"

Lost Worlds
of Memory

1979

THESE LAST WEEKS, as I have been working at my autobiography, I have found the news from Asia giving a special vividness —if only the vividness of contrast—to my memories of the Asian journeys I made during the 1960s, so that the worlds I then visited often seem to me now like worlds lost in the past:

> ... and faiths and empires gleam
> Like wrecks in a dissolving dream.

Trouble flares again in the Lebanon, a few blocks of Beirut become rubble, and I remember the limestone hills crimson with the springtime flowers of anemones that are the blood of the yearly killed Thammuz, and the pseudo-French sophistication of the cafés in downtown Beirut, and the archaeological complexities of Byblos—layer on layer of ancient tyranny, and the antique megalomania of the Baalbek ruins where we went on a day when the roads were patrolled by tanks because even then there were fears of a Syrian invasion and the border was closed so that we could not drive on to Palmyra. Most of all I remember Joseph, our Maronite Christian driver, with his great Phoenician prow of a nose, who at the end of our days together took my wife and me to his house and gathered his Armenian neighbours to join us in a great feast his wife had prepared of all the Lebanese and Syrian delicacies we had talked of as we travelled around the country and had been unable to obtain. I wonder whether Joseph is even alive, and remember his wit and generosity, and the grandeur and peacefulness of the land through which he led us. Though perhaps the relics of invaders we saw even then, from Macedonians and Romans to Arabs and Turks and crusading Franks, should have told us that in the Middle East any appearance of stability is an illusion, that the blood of Thammuz does not flow only in flowers.

Iran breaks apart in conflict; the Shah's rule founders. And again I am remembering, not so much the Germanic urban scape of Teheran, but Isfahan with its great sky-glittering mosques and the intricate dusty warrens of its bazaar; and Shīrāz, where the air seemed sweeter than any other air I had ever breathed and the wine as good as Omar could have drunk; and the tall monuments of Persepolis, with their grave processional sculptures, which (before the Shah had embellished them to make good his claims of being the successor of Cyrus and Darius) stood in stark and little-visited isolation on the edge of the Persian desert. Again people step into my mind. I remember the foreman from an oil rig in Ābādān who stopped us in the bazaar of Shīrāz and insisted on taking us around the town and stopping at booths and eating houses to feed us on the local delicacies, all out of sheer good will and a code of hospitality we found everywhere at work in Iran and which makes the recent outbursts of xenophobia seem so astonishing to me and so far out of the true character of Persians.

Cambodia replaces one disgusting tyranny with another probably almost as bad, and again I remember a land where the social tensions were indeed more evident than they then seemed in Iran or Lebanon, and where the stranger was not so obviously welcome. Yet it was still a land were nobody got killed for political reasons and where the discomforts of travel were caused mainly by a monumental administrative inefficiency, though even then the Khmers of Cambodia struck me as a dourer and far less outgoing people than the neighbouring Thais.

The other day I went looking for my diaries of that period. The notebook on Iran and Lebanon, visited in 1966, seemed to have been lost but I found that for Cambodia, visited in 1964. We had gone there for two purposes: to visit Angkor Wat and the other great Khmer sites in the environs of Siem Reap, and to gather material for a radio documentary on that great chimera of earnest internationalists in the early 1960s, the Mekong River Project, which was expected to bring prosperity to all of Southeast Asia and which has long been washed over by the storms of war.

Cambodia was then still a kingdom, ruled by the regent Prince Sihanouk with an authoritarian caprice that made anyone in authority extremely chary about speaking to strange writers, even when they came, as I did, under United Nations auspices. This accounts for the frustrations that become evident in the diary.

I should explain further that in 1964 Cambodia and Thailand were not on diplomatic speaking terms because of a flare-up in their perennial border disputes. But there were means of travelling between them. One quietly obtained a Cambodian visa at the Indonesian consulate in Bangkok and, though there was theoretically no air communication between the two countries, one of Air Vietnam's flights from Bangkok to Saigon did in fact put down on the way at Phnom Penh, and on the way back to pick up passengers who entered Thailand under the polite fiction that they had come all the way from Vietnam. For the rest, I must leave the reader to form his own picture out of my fleeting impressions of a land that then was open—not without difficulty—to visitors, but now is territory as forbidden as Tibet.

13th February. We arrive at Bangkok Airport at 10:00 A.M. expecting to catch the 10:45 plane to Phnom Penh, but departure is indefinitely postponed with no explanation, since to explain would be publicly to recognize that a landing will be made in Cambodian territory. We do not leave until 3:15 P.M. and only then are we told that the delay has been due to the departure of the president of the Philippines from Cambodia; the airstrip was pre-empted so that the Royal Dancers in their garments of heavy gold brocade could perform their highly stylized dances on the noon-hot asphalt in honour of the departing guest.

The old bucket of a plane gets off the ground with difficulty and sways and totters at low altitudes over the flat rice plains east of Bangkok and over the Cardamom Mountains that lie between Thailand and Cambodia. The heat rising from the ground causes extraordinary bumpiness.

The air hostesses are delectable Annamese girls, with ivory skins and delicate mask faces, dressed in national style—white trousers and long blue silk tunics slit to the waist and high at the neck. But already one is aware of the continuing French presence in Southeast Asia. French is spoken, and fat, sallow French colonials sprawl in the plane seats, drinking the beer whose mild pissy flavour transports one back to the Paris boulevards, as does the flavour of the ice cream with its high water-crystal content.

At Phnom Penh we are met by K.N. of the Mekong Commission, a helpful man with a jeep who takes us to our hotel, hooting his way, as we get near the city's centre, through swarms of cyclo-pousses, which are really cycle rickshaws like those in India except that one sits in front of the driver in a kind of wide wicker basket. There are French shutters and balconies, and trimmed privet hedges before the restaurants that nestle below the apartments, so that downtown Phnom Penh—if it were not for the climate (85° Fahrenheit and maximum humidity) and the predominance of Chinese and Indochinese faces— would pass as a southern French town, somewhere near Montpellier, particularly if one thinks of the magnificent *cours* shaded by old clipped trees, whitewashed to eye level, and the boulevards and monuments of the palace region towards the Mekong River. The people show all levels of sophistication, the poorer women wearing the country dress of the black sampot, a wrap-over skirt worn tightly and reaching to the ground, with a blouse tight over the waist and hips, a coloured cloth wound round the head. Some wealthier women wear Annamese dress, a few Indian women saris. Older men often wear merely a sarong, with no upper covering, and boys often go naked or wear a short open shirt with nothing below.

The hotel has a kind of tropicalized Gallic elegance: a Lurçat tapestry in the bar, orchid trees in the patio, a bidet in the bathroom, and candles with matches, needed later in the evening when there is a power cut of about two hours; this, we gather, happens regularly in Phnom Penh, which has not had a reliable power supply for many years. Prices are high. A soup in the snack bar as a late lunch costs 70 riel each, and the riel is 35 to the dollar.

We wander in streets of nineteenth-century French provincial villas, and only in the market do we get our first flavour of real Cambodian life. The smells strike one first—pungent and half-putrid cooking from the grubby-looking eating stalls, the stench of meat getting high in the afternoon, the strange acrid smell from the warehouses where thousands of dried fish are stacked up like cords of wood. The Cambodians eat most of the fish, the Chinese most of the meat. It is Chinese New Year, the many little stores are decorated with red and gold paper scrolls, and the young Chinese walk the streets in droves and collect outside the Chinese cinemas whose façades are decorated with gigantic cardboard cutout figures of mediaeval warriors and ladies, projecting a bloom of romance that must surely come from Hollywood via Hong Kong rather than from Chinese tradition.

On the plane I told Inge, "Tonight for dinner in Phnom Penh we shall be offered *Tripe à la mode de Caen,*" and she laughed at the absurdity of the idea. But we cross the street from the hotel to have dinner in a French-style restaurant and, sure enough, the *plat du jour* is indeed *Tripe à la mode...*, and all the dishes on the menu follow the French pattern. But my *poulet à la crème* is by no means of French quality, and the greyish-looking baguette harbours tiny red ants, while the Chinese waiter whispers gravely about black market dollars. Later in the evening B., the Cambodian official in charge of negotiations over the Mekong Project, comes to our hotel with his wife. We talk in typical Southeast Asian obliquities about the project, what Cambodia hopes to gain from it. He promises to arrange interviews with the minister, with other officials. He offers, with more confidence, transport into the countryside, help with getting on a plane to Siem Reap, but is in obvious distress when we propose to spend the whole day tomorrow, from 8:00 in the morning to sunset, careering over the Cambodian countryside. At our age, he remarks, it is most unwise. He himself—and his smooth features suggest he is no more than a pampered thirty—always observes the long siesta customary in Phnom Penh. From 1:00 to 3:00, or thereabouts, *on repose*.

14th February. [On this day, the diary records, we go out in the morning to a dam site in arid country west of Phnom Penh, depressed by the infertility of the land, the poverty and obvious sombreness of the people—accentuated by their black garb—after the comparative well-being of Thailand. We come back to the city where the young men who have been our guides take us to the Mondial, a Chinese eating house that probably provides the best food in PP. The prawns are superb, and the ice cream made with coconut milk equally so. At lunch we begin to get our first taste of the Kafka-like elusiveness of Cambodian officialdom. The minister, we are told, has refused to see us; his chief secretary is evasive; B. has retreated into a prolonged siesta. In the afternoon we set off to the site of the great barrage on the Tonle Sap. The Tonle Sap is the channel that connects the Great Lake of Cambodia (also called Tonle Sap in Khmer) with the Mekong; it is a geographical curiosity, a two-way river that, when the Mekong floods in the rainy season, flows upward to fill the Great Lake, and in the dry season flows down to feed the Mekong. The diary recommences.]

We are soon out of Phnom Penh, a small compact town with few suburbs, but a good deal of rather grandiose public building on the outskirts—schools, colleges, housing blocks for government employees, in modern concrete baroque, but often half completed and left for the monsoons to ravage. The country is brown and dried-out; the monsoon rains are heavy, but since the collapse of the Khmer Empire there has been no adequate system of water conservation, and so the moisture runs away, and it is a one-crop land that the Mekong Project could make a three-crop land. Only beside the Tonle Sap, on the swampy verges, are there verdant meadows and, at this season, bright jade green paddies. Close to Phnom Penh, there are small hills with the sharp tips of pagodas rising from their crests, the relics of Oudong, former capital of Cambodia, half buried in the hillside forest. The pagodas are dark and sombre, with none of the gilded glitter of similar structures in Thailand, and drabness, darkness, is what characterizes human settlement here. The houses are undecorated and unpainted boxes on stilts, their wood faded by the monsoons, their roofs silvery—weathered palm thatch—among the palms and the kapok trees—stark candelabra hung with bursting green purses of tree cotton. Even the dress of the people is dark, mostly black, and the only human touches of colour in a Khmer village are the orange robes of the monks at the weatherbeaten wooden temple and the festival decorations on the Chinese stores. The people are darker, more robust than other Southeast Asians, the women very erect, grave in expression; one has the sense of a frustrated and powerful anger, the power that may have built the Khmer Empire. It gains a kind of outlet in the ball games—mainly basketball—that the boys and young men play vigorously in every village during this idle season, clad in ragged shorts or tattered bits of cloth worn kiltwise.

The older men swing in rope hammocks hung in the verandahs of the houses, and the most active people are the Malays who live in some of the villages of the Tonle Sap, have rich-looking mosques, and cycle around the countryside, easily distinguishable by the little white caps they wear. Along the river's edge, between the villages, are wretched little huts, inhabited by workless people who have come out of Phnom Penh to keep alive by fishing the waters that have recently been restocked by the German government. As the afternoon heats up, the people gather around the village wells, the men in sarongs and baretorsoed, the women draping a cloth over their breasts, and spill buckets of water over their bodies and garments for coolness. Burdens are carried always on the head, perched on a scarf tied into a kind of turban, and this I suppose is why the women walk so splendidly.

Our companions, Kon and Lao, have got over their morning shyness; and we talk a great deal, in French (theirs better than ours) and in the GI English they picked up from Americans working a few years ago on the Friendship Highway. Even so, there is little of the outgoing curiosity we found among Thais: a few formal questions like "How many children do you have?" but nothing that betrays a real interest in one or one's way of life. Yet there are odd moments of passion, as when Lao reveals himself a fanatical philatelist, boasting of his hundred albums of stamps, hoping we can keep in touch so that he can get the latest Canadian issues, and Kon raises the rival claims of numismatics and asserts—apocryphally I suspect—that coins of Augustus Caesar have been found at Angkor Thom.

Vestiges of imperialism. The kilometre stones alternate, one in Roman characters, one in Cambodian; the road signs contain both French and Cambodian. Thailand, which evaded the empires, uses only Thai characters on its signs. In the fields beside the Tonle Sap the cows have bells like those used in the French Alps.

The country becomes more arid. There are large coconut groves, embowering the houses, and then low, volcanic-looking conical hills begin to appear on the horizon, and the valley ground is dotted with great squarish boulders, sometimes in piles sixty or seventy feet high, around which the flat alluvial soil laps like a flood. On and on, fading with distance into ever paler blue, continues the succession of low hills, each seeming curiously detached from the one before.

Reach the town of Kampong Chhnang; a provincial capital in French tropical style, with a gardened and balustraded promenade which, at the present time of lowish water, is about twenty feet above the Tonle Sap. From here we see the two converging ranges on each side of the river between which the barrage will be built. Beyond that the ranges diverge to form the wide marshy basin of the Great Lake, which we cannot see now but shall fly over tomorrow. Below the promenade there is a floating village reaching far out into the water, and this is by far the gayest place we have seen in Cambodia, for the houses on the sampanlike boats are gaily painted, like English canal barges, and their little verandahs are decorated with pots of flowering plants. Men from the village are out fishing in midriver from large canoelike boats. Fishing in fact goes on everywhere that water lies. Shallow ponds and even ditches are netted for the small fish that abound there, and in the deeper ponds that are brilliant with beds of blue-flowered water hyacinth and pink-flowered lotus, the people cast with rod and line, for here is where the big fish lurk. The Cambodians are mostly Buddhist and, though they are not happy eating meat, the lives of fish do not seem to lie heavily on their karmas.

We have tea in a French-style café overlooking the river at Chhnang, and eat sugary cakes covered with poisonously dyed icing, and Kon tells about the days when the two old stern-wheelers, beached and decaying near the floating village, provided the only transport to Chhnang and also, through the Great Lake, to Siem Reap and the Angkor complex. Only World War II brought roads that were more than swampy tracks.

Already, at Chhnang, the swamps and lagoons of the Great Lake begin to encroach. There is a great brilliant blue lagoon on the edge of the town, rimmed with the vivid green of meadows and paddies, and here I see a sight that I know immediately will remain for me a symbol of the general human condition in this part of the world. A woman is irrigating her paddy by means of a treadmill waterwheel; she holds on to a bar and tramps away in her long, soiled black sampot, her head sheltered by a conical sunhat, and as the wheel revolves the little bamboo buckets that are attached to it spill their glittering loads of water into the irrigation ditch....

15th February. This morning, when I try to find out about our interviews with Cambodian officials, B. is not even available at his office; clearly he is remaining silent to save face. I go round to the UN office, and D. declares that there is just one reliable official who will not fear to speak to me. He rings up H.P.H., and H.P.H. promises to call at the hotel by 10:30. He does not arrive, and by 12:15, when the airport car arrives to pick us up, he is still not there. Does this portend, as D. thinks the other refusals may, a new outburst by Sihanouk against western countries? Why otherwise are so many officials so anxious to be silent?

Our plane for Siem Reap is supposed to leave at 12:30; in fact, by the time we have gone through the police investigation necessitated by Cambodian "Contrôle de Circulation" regulations, we are not in the air until 2:15, and then, in the antiquated Air Cambodge plane, the air conditioning fails, and as the plane flies over the jungle under a blazing sun, the temperature steadily rises and we drench our clothes with sweat. The Great Lake stretches beneath us, vast and mud-brown, fishing boats scattered like toothpicks over its surface, and then the plane is circling over the great mass of Angkor Wat, its high towers piercing up from the surrounding jungle, and down to the Siem Reap airport. Another police inspection. Then, at the hotel, we find Air Cambodge has not booked a room for us. An arrogant French manager declares there is nothing he will do for us. Do we expect him to put up a tent on the lawn? Since we know that the hotel near the temples has been taken over by the crew filming *Lord Jim,* we and the six other people in the same boat declare we will doss down in the lounge. An hour later, rooms are quietly found, we have tea, and then get a cyclo-pousse to see Angkor Wat in the evening light. The driver pedals down the straight hot road into the jungle, the trees growing taller and the undergrowth thicker; out of it sounds a ringing by some cicada-like creature that in unison falls and then rises to an almost deafening loudness. We reach the square moat, with the first of the concentric walls of the temple on the far side. Small boys are swimming, water buffalo graze on weeds and lift their heads out of the water like primeval monsters, flocks of water birds float among the leaves of giant water lilies, a trio of elephants employed on *Lord Jim* are being driven by their mahouts into the moat, and a little way down from the causeway there are pile dwellings of bamboo, actually standing in midwater, with dugouts moored to their supports.

The driver leaves us at the beginning of the causeway, and we walk over the moat, and through the arch on to the second causeway; now we get our first view of the temple itself, so far down the pavement of worn stones, with its serpent balustrades, that only as we approach do we realize its real magnitude. It is a successive unfolding of surprises, large and small wonders. The great relief carvings of scenes from the Ramayana on the outer wall of the temple itself; the collection of Khmer Buddhas, some of them crumbling wood, in a side gallery used as a depository; the towers in whose dark corbelled heights the big bats squeak and flutter and drop their dung, which gives the air a sour odour. The tide of visitors is already ebbing. A few Frenchmen from Phnom Penh, a young Portuguese who talks to us, a fanatical little Japanese photographer are all that remain. Half a dozen gentle-faced young monks flit in the corridors, their orange robes like flames in the dusk, and three small boys cling around us, trying to take our hands and pull us up the stairs, beating their chests to draw attention to themselves.

We climb the final flight of steps, as steep as those of a Mexican pyramid, to the uppermost platform, and look down over the complex pattern of steep-edged roofs, their grey mottled with the darker patterns of lichen, a mandala in stone, a manmade holy Mount Meru. We see the village to the north of the temple, cane huts half-hidden by the ragged banners of banana leaves, bare-torsoed men walking in from the fields, and a small modern temple with a bronze bell ringing. It is the best hour for Angkor Wat, all the time the light changing and more deeply gilding the grey stone, and the patterns of light and shadow moving over the sculptured walls, until, as we return across the causeway, we look back and see the last patch of sunlight fading off the façade and leaving the great temple standing as a dark but somehow still glowing mass against the brilliant sky. As we drive back, the sides of the moat are filled with people taking their evening bath, naked boys glistening with moisture run shouting beside us, and looking back we see the richness of the afterglow concentrated in the orange robes of a group of monks standing on the causeway.

16th February. Set out at 8:00 in the hotel bus to see Angkor Thom, the great city of the Khmers, in the morning freshness. Our fellow passengers—a professor and his wife from California, writing a book about concepts of landscape over 2000 years; an aged, retired Indian civil servant, bird-thin, with panama hat, hearing aid, cine-camera and solicitous younger wife; a Peruvian couple, probably diplomats; a Canadian woman who works with Foster Parents in Saigon; a frayed American newspaperman from Tokyo; a nice old English lady who a century ago would have daringly gone to Sicily; and two American businessmen with intellectual interests. The Japanese fill another bus and keep to themselves.

We drive past the moat of Angkor Wat, the tower of the temple shining silvery brilliant in the early light. Then in at the great south gate of Angkor Thom; rows of kneeling gods and demons support the long snake balustrades of the causeway, and on each side of the gate tower a massive enigmatically smiling face of Brahma looks out over the ruined world of the Khmers. Inside the gate we ride into jungle, where the long-decayed wooden palaces and houses of the city stood, to the great stone mass of the central temple of Bayon. At this hour the mass of towers rising one above the other to the central sanctuary takes on a curious insubstantiality of appearance, caused partly by the hazy morning softness of the jungle light and partly by the soft blue-greens of the lichens that creep over its stones. The effect is so subtle that the great faces on the towers—similar to those on the gate—seem to be materializing out of the rock, growing into shape, rather than having been faded back into it by the wearing of time. When we pass by again, just before noon, in the hard light of midday, all this magic has vanished.

Bayon has drains as elaborate as those of Cretan palaces, and much low-relief carving of filigree delicacy in which little Buddhas appear among acanthuslike foliage that suggests the remote influence of the Greek Buddhist artists of Gandhara. But there is nothing Greek about the great masks on the towers or the people who take part in the battles by land and water recorded on the major friezes of Bayon. These faces are undeniably Khmer, spiritualized in the greater godly form, earthy and very much like the people we have been seeing about Siem Reap in the warriors and the rowers of the ships that move through rippling water where crocodiles and great fishes lurk.

Boys surround us outside Bayon, selling knives, bows and arrows, the bamboo bells with teak clappers used on the cattle here. There is soft shrill music—boys playing bamboo flutes and one-string fiddles, a woman selling green coconuts who plays a melodious little bamboo jew's-harp to attract customers.

We go on via the Elephant Terrace and the Garuda Terrace, named after their dominant reliefs, to the site of the Khmer kings' palace; nothing except the terraces and two large baths is left, for the palace was built of wood and the Thais burnt it. The destructive attacks of the Thais were one of the reasons why the great complex of Angkor Thom was abandoned. After it ceased to be capital of the Khmer Empire, people drifted away except for a few monkish hermits and a few hunters; the jungle embraced the ruins, which became the haunt of monkeys, tigers, wild elephants, who used the monuments as rainy season shelters. A further irony of imperialism: just as British archaeologists gave back to Indians the past they now treasure, so French archaeologists uncovered the Khmer past and pieced together its history....

After lunch we hire a motorcycle rickshaw to visit as many of the outlying jungle temples as we can in a long afternoon. The driver a ragged older man, with grey hair, sunken toothless cheeks, very dark skin. The noon sun pelts down, but the speed of the rickshaw relieves the heat as we pass the moat of Angkor Wat and turn off on jungle paths that lead us to Banteay Kdei, the first of the temples that dot the jungle north of the Great Lake. Walk in through the Brahma-faced gate, up the winding path—swept clear so that snakes can be seen—through the high jungle, over the moat lush with lilac-blue water lilies over which hover giant red dragonflies. As we enter the temple copper-coloured lizards scuttle over the stone lions beside the door. A line of receding square arches stretches before us, in the centre a Buddha illuminated by the sunlight falling into the innermost court. We pass through the chambers. One contains a stone lingam, another a miniature pagoda seven feet high. There are other Buddhas, headless, with little holes in the necks into which joss sticks have been thrust; every recognizable image indeed seems the object of continued worship. Moss and vivid ferns grow in the damper corners of the chambers; there are many bats, and once we catch the strong musky odour of some animal—perhaps a civet—that makes its lair here.

The temple has never been completely cleared of jungle, and at the west end the ficus trees still clamber on top of the walls, roots reaching down like root hands in a surrealist painting. The feeling in the collapsing courts at this end is melancholy and slightly menacing.

On to the temple of Ta Prohm, a few kilometres of jungle road away. Here the jungle is even thicker, and the ruins have never been liberated from its grasp. The midday air is sullen and breathless, and the noise is incessant as the insects trill, the jungle cocks crow, the doves croon, the coppersmith birds tap, and other birds chatter and sing. Dry teak leaves fall crisply around us. Here the buttressed roots of the ficus trees are gigantic, and other forms of life seem to correspond, for we find a snail shell three inches across. It is hard to describe the broken chaos of Ta Prohm with the trees sending down roots like great pythons, breaking down the roofs and walls with their weight and prising the massive blocks apart into moss-covered piles of rubble. Everywhere in the collapsing chambers one hears the rustle and flicker of bat wings. Ant heaps top the walls. Spiders have constructed strange webs that funnel into tubes of gossamer at whose end the spiders sit waiting. The dry skin of a large snake flutters like limp cellophane. Monkeys chatter invisibly in the treetops. The light filters through the top of a broken tower on to a worn reclining Buddha, and a rusty tin before it is filled with flowers. Perhaps they were put there by the old, bare-torsoed man we saw sitting on a step when we came in and who follows us in curiosity. As we leave the temple two women jog by on the jungle path carrying heavy baskets on yokes, and other women are going among the trees with hatchets and bamboo buckets, evidently gathering some kind of gum. A small boy who is with them spies us and runs up. "Smoke, papa!" he shouts at me, miming the action of puffing a cigarette.

[The diary describes visits to half a dozen other temples, pyramids, a great artificial lake constructed by the Khmer kings for irrigation, and return to the Grand Hotel. It continues.]

Snack of iced tea, Gruyère sandwiches, good English cake. Walk beside the river into the town of Siem Reap. In the river boys are swimming, supported by bundles of green reeds like the *cabellitos de totora* used on the coast of Peru, and great waterwheels, elaborately constructed of bamboo, are slowly turning in the stream and feeding the irrigation ditches. The day's market is almost over in the village square, the poor people walking home with little bundles of fish bought cheaply at the end of the day, but the open-air Chinese restaurants are still doing business, and the shops around the square are open: they sell some rather beautiful olive-green stoneware and nice Chinese-style blue-and-white, richly coloured and designed cloths for festival sampots and sarongs, baskets of many kinds; a native pharmacist has a stall with such curiosities as a sawfish's sword, cats' furs, gigantic dried fungi, dried starfish, etc. Drink Vermouth Cassis in evening light in little Frenchified Chinese restaurant and walk back to Grand Hotel as night falls with tropical quickness, like a curtain....

18th February. Back in Phnom Penh. Visit D. again at UN. Agrees we have used up possibilities of an official interview. Talks bitterly of Sihanouk. "A terrible fellow, always mocking his ministers and subordinates, always changing governments. His top men are overworked and the small fry are scared into paralysis." As a consolation D. arranges for us to see the palace and loans us a UN car. An old steward in a white suit takes us round. The queen, Sihanouk's mother, lives there, but there is no longer a crowned king. The palace is new, built within the past fifty years, in something one might call Cambodian Lutyens, mingling French Third Republic grandiosity with traditional Indochinese themes. There are vast parade grounds, and in one of the pavilions a crude mural of the Ramayana, which confirms one's impression that what passes now for a Cambodian culture is the faintest shadow of the past. Most interesting is the royal regalia, with all it suggests of a past of semi-divine kingship. The four coronation crowns—for the throne, for the litter, for riding on horseback, for riding on elephant back. The heavy cloth-of-gold garments, different for each stage of the ceremony, that must be stifling in such a climate. The throne, the bed where the king lies briefly in state, gilded like the beds of Tutankhamen. The gold (right) and silver (left) mats on which the king places his feet when washing. The sword of state. The household deities, Hindu as well as Buddhist. The funeral chariot, and the golden basket for washing the king's ashes with coconut milk after cremation. Most astonishing of all the Cambodian emblems of royalty, an ordinary black bowler hat with a diamond knob attached to the top, and on one side a jewelled cockade with a 40-carat diamond in the centre!

From one of the halls, the sound of a gamelan orchestra, gongs and strings. "It is the Royal Dancers, practising," says the old man. We are anxious to watch. "Impossible, monsieur! The queen is supervising the rehearsal. No one else can be present."

Chinese New Year is over, the town returning to normal, all the shops open and men sitting on chairs outside them when we go out in the evening, with Australian engineers from the Mekong Project, to eat at the Mondial. Excellent crab and noodle soup, succulent beignets of prawn, crisp fried wun tun; the best food yet in Southeast Asia.

19th February. Fly back to Bangkok. It has rained, and as we drive from the airport the landscape glistens joyfully with the unexpected moisture. We tell the travel agent of our frustrations in Phnom Penh. She laughs. "Now you will know why we feel as we do about the Cambodians! We may look a little like each other, but we are completely different people!"

Seven
Burmese Days

1983

I FIRST SET out for Burma in January 1964. With some difficulty, since the First Secretary in the Delhi Embassy suspected my intentions as a writer, I had got a visa for a ten-day visit. General Ne Win had staged his military coup d'état just over a year before, and the Burmese government was sensitive about potentially critical visitors. Leaving Delhi, my wife and I flew to Dacca, in what was then East Pakistan, and then went on to Chittagong near the Burmese border, intending to spend a few days there visiting the Buddhist tribesmen of the Chittagong Hill Tracts and afterwards fly on to Rangoon.

Chittagong was—and I gather still is—one of the most dismal places in the world, a sink of irremediably squalid poverty and a fair competitor for the title of *rectum mundi*. After two days we decided to hurry up our trip to Burma. But by the time we got to the airlines office, the Burmese government had abruptly cancelled all visas. No tourists were to be allowed into the country. Rather than spend any longer in Chittagong, where our arrangements to visit the hill tribes had broken down, we flew back that day to Calcutta and caught a connecting plane to Bangkok. All we saw of Burma on that trip took up a few virtuoso lines in my book *Asia, Gods and Cities*.

Night fell at double speed as we sped towards the darkness, and when the clouds cleared on the verge of land, Burma lay in shadow beneath us, deep blue outlined against the lighter sea, while the sky was still intensely luminous. We saw the great rivers in streaks of pallor running through the obscurity of the jungles, and the spreading circles of fire as the peasants burnt off their paddies. The sun dropped suddenly out of the western sky like a light going out, and the colours of the horizon changed quickly from orange, through lemon and lime to a lucid aquamarine, and then, by a curious lapse in the prismatic succession, shifted to violet and through indigo to the dark blue of night. Through that night we flew over the borders of the land that had been forbidden to us and descended at Bangkok into the dense, caressing darkness of Siam.

At Calcutta, on our way, we had gained a good idea why we and all other transient foreigners were being kept out of Burma. As we waited for our connection at Dum Dum airport, a Thai Airlines plane landed, and shortly afterwards the passengers began to trail raggedly across the tarmac to the airport building. They were all Indians: old men in dhotis and young men in cheap suits; women in gaudy saris and children of all ages. Each of the adults carried a bundle of umbrellas, and the trolleys that followed them were laden with the bedrolls that accompany all Indian travellers, some of them gaping open so that their contents spilled out onto the asphalt. There was no possible doubt of their status; they had the peculiar numb look of refugees the world over.

We soon found that they were Indians being expelled from Burma. Their fathers and grandfathers had gone there during the nineteenth century in the wake of the British conquerors. Some had never been more than coolies, but the merchants among them had prospered, engrossed most of the retail business in Burma that the Chinese did not already own, acquired a great deal of land, and in the process had become even more resented than the British themselves.

Seven Burmese Days

A "Burma for the Burmese" policy was one of the ways in which Ne Win and the new military government calculated to gain popularity, and since there is a long record of mild xenophobia in Burma, they were probably right in their calculations. So, as part of a general nationalization of businesses, hundreds of thousands of Indians were stripped of their livelihood and packed out of the country with what they could carry, in the same way as their compatriots some years later in Kenya and Uganda.

Since witnesses would be inconvenient, foreign visitors were kept out, and the ban, once constituted, lasted for many years, years during which Burma seemed to withdraw from the world, all through the sixties and long into the seventies, to nurse the wounds of its own disunity as Ne Win and his army strove in vain to suppress the guerrilla forces of various kinds that in the worst periods occupied as much as half of the country. A deliberate and lengthy attempt was made to keep out foreign visitors, foreign ideas and influences, foreign products and foreign trade. Burma proclaimed itself a socialist country and followed the communist pattern by establishing the rule of a single party, the Burma Socialist Programme Party. But it remained aloof—even hostilely aloof—from Russia and China, both of which were supporting communist guerrilla bands in its eastern and northern hill regions.

Burma's withdrawal lasted for a decade or so, thanks largely to its dwindling self-sufficiency in such basic products as rice, fish and petroleum, until the need for foreign currency, foreign technologies, even some forms of foreign education made it open its frontiers once again during the 1970s. I still wanted to see Burma, partly because of George Orwell's connection with the country (he served in the Indian Imperial Police there and wrote *Burmese Days* out of the experience) and partly because of the splendid ruins of the great mediaeval Buddhist centre of Pagan on the Irrawaddy between Rangoon and Mandalay. But it was only this year that a trip to India (to write a book on the country in collaboration with Toni Onley, the painter) gave me the chance to make the visit to Burma I had planned two decades before.

To the traveller in the early 1980s Burma still looks at first sight like the tight little country my experience years before had led me to expect. Burma's peculiar shape, like a sting ray with a diamond-shaped body and a long tail running down beside Thailand, gives it long frontiers in relation to its area, which is a little more than that of Alberta. But no one is allowed to cross the frontiers by land, largely because the government is not everywhere in control of these regions. The only way travellers can in fact enter is by plane, usually from Bangkok to Rangoon. One's reception, with elaborate currency and customs forms and a showy if inefficient examination of baggage, fits the picture of a strictly controlled situation, as does the fact that visas are restricted to a week and only limited parts of the country are open to visitors—mainly the Irrawaddy valley with a few outlying places like Maymyo, Moulmein and Inle Lake. Finally, it is only possible to get around the country with the help and under the surveillance of Tourist Burma, the state corporation that is the equivalent of Intourist. Apart from anything else, Tourist Burma controls the hotels, and its charter planes are the only reliable means of transport in a situation where the shortness of one's stay makes every day precious.

But what we found, when we travelled up to the dusty former capital of Mandalay, and down to the half-desert of Pagan where the remains of five thousand ancient pagodas crumble among the thorn trees, and spent the days we had left talking to the people we were able to meet in Rangoon, was a much more flexible and pluralist society than we had envisaged, resembling not the closed box of our expectations so much as a colander, rigid in structure but full of holes.

It is true that Burma is in name a socialist commonwealth ruled by a single party, in which elections serve only as tests of loyalty, since failure to turn out and vote for the sole candidate is likely to bring the police to one's door. There is a political police, reportedly trained by East German experts, but if I can judge from the two agents who on different occasions rather obtrusively listened to our conversations in Rangoon hotels, it seems to be rather gauche in its operations. And there is a network of unobtrusive organizations by which the government hopes to keep tabs on ordinary people, like the fire guard whose squads drill of an evening in the back lanes of Rangoon. The excuse for the fire guard is the great inflammability of the split bamboo huts in which many Burmese live even in the city, but in practice it tends to serve as an auxiliary to the police.

The Burma Socialist Programme Party is in fact little more than a front for an army rule that still continues in fact if not in name. Many of the ministers in the so-called civilian government are in fact former army officers who resigned their ranks in order to fill governmental posts, and though the presidency of the country is now in the hands of a carefully chosen political nonentity, General Ne Win, who remains chairman of the Socialist Programme Party, still virtually controls the government. And through its seven administrative divisions of the Burma-inhabited lowlands and its seven tribal states, subdivided into more than two hundred township administrations, the government theoretically enmeshes the whole of Burma.

But much of this administrative structure exists only on paper, and being in control of the government does not in Burma mean being in control of the country. At no time since Burma became independent in 1948 has the administration in Rangoon ruled the whole of it. Even today it effectively controls only the area inhabited by Burmans, about 70 per cent of the population. The rest of the country—almost half the area—is either permanently or intermittently under the control of insurgents who represent a variety of causes. Some are communist-oriented, inclining to Moscow or Peking; others, in Shan State especially, are deeply involved in the drug traffic of the Golden Triangle; yet others are devoted to ethnic autonomy, like the Karen rebels, who have so long been in control of areas on the frontier of Thailand that they now have elaborate administrations complete with advanced educational and health services. Adequate for policing the flat lands, the Burmese army is ill-equipped for fighting in the jungle-clad hill areas, though this situation may change if the United States sends in equipment under the pretext of helping suppress the opium-based drug trade that passes through Shan territory.

This situation, and the weakness it represents, have helped to shape the policies of the Burmese government, which in several important ways have differed from those of authoritarian socialist governments in countries like Russia and China, Vietnam and Cambodia. Though the land was nationalized under U Nu's administration, even before Ne Win's coup d'état, the tendency had been towards encouraging co-operation among the individual peasants who still work their own holdings rather than collectivization, and because this fits in with the traditionally communal elements in Burmese village life, it has been relatively successful, though bureaucratic confusion at higher levels has created problems of food distribution.

Also, unlike the Russian and Chinese administrations, the Burmese Socialist Programme Party had never dared to act against religion. The influence of the Sangha, the Buddhist order of monks to which almost every male Burman belongs for a period in his young manhood, is symbolized by the vast bell-shaped Shwe Dagon Pagoda, whose great stupa, covered thickly with real gold and surrounded by eighty lesser but equally resplendent shrines, towers and glitters over the decayed colonial streets of modern Rangoon, where little has been built or even renovated since the British left in 1948. Every day at the Shwe Dagon, and at the almost equally resplendent downtown Sule Pagoda, hundreds of people throng the peripheral bazaars and worship at the shrines. Often they are in family groups, offering crimson and gold bunches of highly stylized artificial flowers and pouring water over the images of the Buddha. The latter function is performed only by the men, watched by the kneeling women and children. There is certainly male privilege in Burmese Buddhism, for the nuns are much poorer and less regarded than the monks, and no women—not even nuns—are allowed on the upper terrace of the Shwe Dagon, which is reserved for men to meditate and pray to the sweet tinklings of the tiny golden bells on the pagodas, shifted by the wind.

In some ways, particularly in their puritanism, Theravada Buddhism and Burmese socialism seem to fit in well together, and many of the laws tend to be distinctly puritanical. For example, it is forbidden to play cards or to dance so that bodies in any way touch. Birth control and any advocacy of it are also forbidden, but this has political and demographic reasons; with its 34 million people and lengthy shared borders with the world's most populous countries, China and India, the Burmese government is anxious to increase the population as a whole and also to sustain the proportion of Burmans to that of the smaller ethnic groups whose loyalty is so unreliable.

Whether or not it is due to the influence of Buddhism, the Burmese socialist-military dictatorship has certainly a less ferocious record than that of other military or authoritarian socialist states. There have indeed at various periods been widespread detentions of potential dissidents, and I met several journalists who freely discussed their periods of imprisonment. But I caught no hint of mass atrocities like those perpetrated in Russia under Stalin or in nearby Cambodia more recently under Pol Pot. That kind of fanaticism, with its desire for the total physical elimination of opponents, does not seem to be part of the Burmese temperament, even among the military classes.

This inclination seems to have a great deal to do with the way in which Burma's curtain of isolation is steadily being weakened by the penetration of western influences. One of the reasons for this, or rather perhaps one of the accompanying circumstances, has been the virtual collapse of the attempt to create a centralized state-dominated economy. Theoretically the main suppliers of goods are the stores that the government operates everywhere, and the privately run stores in the markets are supposed to play a marginal role in distribution. In practice, one finds that the government stores, like those in Russia, are often short of essential items. But there never seems to be any shortage in the stalls that operate in the big downtown markets of cities like Rangoon and Mandalay, and now the black market—euphemistically referred to as the "open market"—has a tacitly recognized place in the Burmese economy. One can walk into Scott Market, right behind the big half-empty government stores, and find western goods of every kind offered without any attempt at concealment, from electronic equipment to whiskey, and from cosmetics to chocolate.

Some of these goods come in small boats from southern Thailand and from Penang in Malaysia. Kipling's Moulmein, on the coast south of Rangoon, is a key centre, and there is a point outside Rangoon where the daily train from Moulmein, popularly known as the Smuggler's Express, suddenly erupts with bundles thrown from windows to be picked up by accomplices before the train reaches the capital. Another route is overland from Chiang Mai in northern Thailand, where the border is held by Karen rebels, who charge a flat 5 per cent on goods passing through their territory and in this way equip themselves with the modern weapons that enable them to defy Ne Win's army. This is the route used by the gem smugglers. Theoretically the gem trade is a government monopoly, and the visitor is supposed to buy the famous Burmese rubies for inflated prices at official "Diplomatic Shops." But many European gem dealers enter the country as tourists, meet the black-market dealers, pick out their stones, leave the country with clean baggage, and in Thailand travel to Chieng Mai where a courier who has crossed the border with the help of the Karens meets them with the gems they have purchased.

The result of this double economy is a situation in which covert exists beside overt prosperity. The overtly prosperous are the high army officers and government officials, who ride in the large black Mercedes and Mazdas for which every humbler car driver draws to the side of the road. Their wealth is as carelessly ostentatious as that of high Russian commissars. Those who gain wealth unofficially follow a low profile style that allows them a degree of freedom and prosperity as long as they keep up the right appearances. Never to display one's means unnecessarily is the cardinal rule. That is why the elaborately balconied apartment blocks of Rangoon are so depressingly seedy on the outside, no matter how many elegant interiors they conceal. That is why a man with an attractive property lets the bushes and weeds run wild on the frontage; his property is less likely to be requisitioned by a passing general who takes a fancy to it. That is why one of the best Chinese restaurants outside China serves its paradisaical seafoods to diplomats and Burmese intellectuals on plastic-covered tables in shabby booths. If the Good Soldier Schweik lives anywhere in the modern world, he is a citizen of Burma: a middle-class citizen of Burma.

For under the level of covert and overt prosperity, of military commissars and black marketeers, lies that great mass of the Burmese poor, whose per capita income as recently as 1977 was only $115 a year. In vast areas of rural Burma people live in a mainly subsistence economy, using little cash. Elsewhere their full-time earnings are often minimal. In small-town communities like Pagan I found men working, splitting bamboos into thin strips for house walls or carrying out the intricate stages of lacquering, at seven to ten kyats a day, which on the official exchange is $1.00 to $1.50 and in the black market from 40 to 55 cents. Down the road at Pagan in the hotel run by the government for tourists the room boys were getting ten kyats a day and hoping for tips that were officially forbidden. I never actually saw anyone in Burma looking as destitute as the poorest Indians; I never encountered beggars other than the monks and nuns who were mendicants to acquire religious merit. But real poverty exists there and a proof of its existence is that, as well as "birth control," one of the forbidden words in Burma is "malnutrition." By government decree, malnutrition does not exist and therefore cannot be discussed; as one doctor remarked to me, the wise public servant disguises his concern by talking about "the need to find the right balance among the freely available sources of nutrition." Not inappropriately, it was in Burma that George Orwell began to learn about doubletalk.

Encounters with India

1983

THE DESERT SHIFTS from stone to sand and back to stone, and then to sand again, windswept dunes with a haze in the air from the blown-up dust. The vegetation becomes a tussocky herbage, rather like sagebrush, that barely holds the sand, and the edges of the road are blurred by the drifting dunes. The colour of the dunes shades off from yellow to mauve and rose and back to yellow.

We are now almost two hundred miles beyond the already remote Rajput town of Bikaner, at the end of a long, slow day of driving, our eyes sore from the sun, our throats grated by the dust. The aged Ambassador bucks and rattles on the narrow road chewed up by military convoys, and with difficulty I scribble on my pad scattered words, a mad shorthand that I hope I can interpret for my journal at the end of the day. Toni Onley, the artist, sitting beside me, is unable to sketch and so soaks in the colour with his eyes, waiting for the endless fidgeting motion to stop so that he can trap it all in paint.

The desert continues, sand and stone and sand, broken by small sights that in the monotony take on the shining self-sufficiency of surrealist images. The picked-over skeleton of a bullock by the roadside, white Brahmini kites prising off the last morsels. A gazelle buck staring at the car from fifteen feet away, then doing a leaping turn to bound away over the desert. A herd of camels—perhaps a hundred—guarded by two small boys as they crop the wretched scrub. A friezelike procession of women, red pots balanced on their heads, walking over the sand to a village whose round storage huts look like Basuto kraals and whose little cubical houses with smoothed mud walls could have been lifted from anywhere in the Sahara. The women's shawls and wide skirts are bright red, orange, yellow—the colours of survival in the desert; they wear heavy silver anklets above their bare feet and tiers of ivory bracelets on their upper arms. Around the village bits of roughly tilled ground, too ragged to be called fields, are being watered laboriously by men in immense red turbans from wells where oxen draw up great leather buckets; they seem to grow nothing but millet, the crop of a rainless land. No rain has fallen here, a shepherd told us, for four years.

It all seems as if it will never end. There is only one road over the Thar Desert of Rajasthan, and eventually we top a small rise and suddenly, perhaps four miles away in the midst of the flatness, see the great outcrop, long and flat topped, on which the city of Jaisalmer grows, like some vast mollusk lit by the late afternoon sun, with the spires of its nine Jain temples gleaming against the hard enamel-blue of the sky.

We let out a great thirsty cry as the camel men must have done through the long centuries when the great caravans trod this way from Persia through Baluchistan and the desert of Sind, eastward to the Great Moghul's capital in Delhi. Surjeet, our driver, pulls his Sikh beard, gives a thankful salaam to the decal of Guru Nanak on the windshield and puts his foot on the gas to speed down the long hill and land us at the spartan little tourist bungalow under the city walls to wet our whistles with tall bottles of Golden Eagle beer before we enter the great gateway to the town.

Jaisalmer is India's Ultima Thule, the last city to the northwest, less than sixty-five miles from where the dunes merge without a break into Pakistan. Its Rajput rulers grew rich on the tolls they charged the caravans, and the city filled with merchants who built the Jain temples and crammed the space within the walls with their mansions, or *halevis*. Only in the present century did a light railway reach Jaisalmer; the road we followed was built much later, after India became independent in 1947 and the old native principalities, of which Jaisalmer was one, were incorporated into the new republic. There is still no airstrip and nothing nearer a hotel than the tourist bungalow, where big-eared desert rats roam the building at night and the only meals are hot, enormous curries. The bungalow was not full; there are still few travellers who endure the journey by night train from Jodhpur or the two days of desert driving from Jaipur via Bikaner that we had just completed.

In other ways than a lack of tourists Jaisalmer's remoteness had kept it less changed than most other Indian places in the 1980s. Travelling through Jaipur on our way there, we found that once-quiet little princely city, where in 1961 I went about by pony-drawn carts because cabs were so few, transformed into a busy state capital of one million inhabitants. The only refuge from the noise and stench was now the great enclosure of the City Palace. A day onward, in Bikaner, the Edwardian age was slowly dying among the brass beds and steel engravings of the rooms in the Lall Garh Palace, which had been turned into a hotel, but here too the present was intruding, in the big, new camps on the sandy edges of the city, with old British orders shouted on the dusty parade grounds and new Russian guns and tanks squatting under great camouflage nets in the desert.

Lack of water saved Jaisalmer from expanding like the other cities; only recently was piped water brought in from artesian wells among the dunes, and not much of it, so there are few new buildings in Jaisalmer, and almost all of them are outside the great wall around which the traffic circles. The streets inside the gates are mostly too narrow and in the upper parts too steep to be more than walkways; in Jaisalmer, as in Venice, the sound of footsteps is always in one's ears.

It was Arthur Erickson, the Vancouver architect, who first urged me to go to Jaisalmer; he had never seen a city, he said, more magically "all of a piece." All of a piece it certainly was, for the whole city was built of the same golden stone as the walls. On the outside it formed the massive blocks of the round bastions. On the inside it was carved into the geometries of stone that covered the walls of mansions and small houses alike and filled the lattices of the floating balconies with screens that looked like rigid lace. In every street the stone carvers had been at work, making the kind of airy, shady houses needed for the heat of the desert, and at the same time creating whole streets and cities of architectural gems that were not deserted monuments but places where Rajput people still lived. The princes had gone, but the feel of the princely past was still strong: in the temples filled with hundreds of rigid Jain images where priests in orange robes appeared out of the incense-smelling shadows to direct one to the nearest money chest of brass-bound teak; in the bazaars of little smoky shops where spices and dyes were laid out in brilliant pyramids and silversmiths sat weighing their heavy peasant jewellery, which they sold by weight rather than by artistry, which was still taken for granted; most of all, in the square high up in the citadel, with the façade of the palace—covered with balconies like rococo swallows' nests—on one side, and on the other, a kind of Greek theatre of tiered stone benches from which the maharajah would hold durbars sitting on the marble throne that remained on the top level.

As in most of India, it was the Jaisalmer women who seemed to keep the traditions most faithfully. A girl in a doorway of filigreed stone, in her brilliant mirrored skirt, with a gold-edged red mantle drawn over her head, looked exactly like a princess waiting for her lover in one of those exquisite eighteenth-century miniatures that used to be painted in the courts of Rajput cities like Jaisalmer. Some of the men also kept to past ways; an old man walked beside me in a brocade jacket and white jodhpurs and told me that his son was a professor of agriculture in an Ontario college. But most of them—especially the kind of men we bargained with in furtive upper rooms over silver jewellery and camel-bone bracelets masquerading as ivory—compromised shabbily between past and present, wearing old suit coats with muslin dhotis and white Gandhi caps instead of big, bright Rajput turbans.

Only the children in Jaisalmer had slipped entirely into the modern age. They clustered excitedly around us, anxious to touch, to hold our hands, not begging for money, but shouting, "One pen! One bonbon!" They were being prepared for the future when all we saw around us would be changed, when the planned airport would be opened and the big, new hotel built on the site already marked out for it. A boy greeted me in German: "*Guten Morgen, mein Herr.*" A girl excitedly warned Inge, my wife, in French not to have anything to do with the two boys who spoke smooth English, told us that in high school they were being taught tourism as a subject and offered themselves as guides for the sake of practice. We accepted; they were informed and resourceful and at the end refused any payment except a treat of Kwality ice cream and a couple of Bic pens.

In Jaisalmer I felt again the sense of discovery and newness that, when I first visited India more than twenty years ago, I had experienced almost everywhere in the country. That first time, in 1961, what impressed and delighted me was the diversity and unpredictability of experience wherever we went, in cities as well as villages, on the main trunk roads as much as in the remote areas where roads hardly existed.

India has fourteen main languages and regional cultures corresponding to them, but the local variations of tradition and custom were far more numerous than that, and in 1961, only fourteen years after liberation, they had survived Moghul rule and the British Raj with a surprisingly pristine vitality. I used to tell my friends when I came back from such journeys: "There's one infallible rule about travel in India. It's never boring, for when you go to bed at night there'll be something new and surprising and interesting to encounter." And I was telling the truth as I knew it then. My first book on the country, *Faces of India,* was filled with the daily detail of wonders and oddities, strange sights seen and strange things heard in a land where local cultures flourished and the homogenizing forces of the twentieth century still moved very slowly. Coming back this past winter from our last visit to India, I reread that book with near astonishment. What I had been telling my friends for twenty years suddenly seemed a lie when I applied it to present-day India. Towns such as Jaisalmer, it seemed to me, were now the exceptional places, which by some accident of bad communications had preserved their architectural integrity still unbroken, their people, apart from a little native rascality, still unspoilt.

Indeed, I found this last encounter with India so disturbing that it took me weeks to get in the mood for writing about it, not because travel was any more difficult than it had ever been, nor because we encountered hostility (which was as rare as it had ever been in the past). It was something far deeper, which can possibly best be described in erotic similes, comparing it to the feeling of a man who has nursed a passion for a third of his life and finds that he is falling out of love, which, of course, is a different thing from falling into hatred, for falling out of love is contingent on the sense of identification that has made one fall into love. One can be out of love, robbed of illusion, and still in agonized connection.

India had entered my mind and blood. For a long period, through the sixties and well into the seventies, Inge and I would go there every other year, for months at a time. We became, so far as one can in these post-Raj days, old India hands. I wrote five books and innumerable articles derived from what I saw there. We spent a good deal of time in those years raising money to resettle the Tibetan refugees who had come down into India with the Dalai Lama in 1959. Many of my friends, outside as well as in the country, were and still are Indians and Tibetans; the oldest such relationship dates back long before my arrival in India, to the early 1940s, when I got to know in London the novelist Mulk Raj Anand, who in turn introduced me to George Orwell. In the middle seventies, travel in other parts of the world and personal problems prevented us from continuing the journeys to India, but we kept our interest, reading books on the country as they came out, reacting with mild fury to the negativism of V. S. Naipaul's *An Area of Darkness* (itself a tale of frustrated love) and with disquiet admiration to Salman Rushdie's *Midnight's Children,* and keeping up our friendships, one of which in the end drew us back.

Patwant Singh is an Indian writer and the editor of *Design,* India's best architectural magazine. His father was one of the Sikh contractors who, under the direction of Sir Edwin Lutyens, built the dramatic complex of rose-coloured stone buildings in the heart of New Delhi that was designed to enshrine the authority of the British Raj and is now the node of power in independent India. We met Patwant in 1961, an hour after our first landing in Bombay, and in a week he and Mulk Raj Anand between them had introduced us to all the local literati, artists and filmmakers, giving enormous parties to which everyone came.

His social adeptness and his love of pleasure made one think of Patwant as an intelligent playboy, capable of writing a good book on Indian politics and picking a good tailor on Savile Row, of editing an elegant magazine and wearing his highly starched turban in just as elegant combination with his Gucci shoes, but skittering rather lightly over the tragic aspects of existence.

About four years ago, all this changed dramatically, as it does often with Indian men who approach the darker verges of middle age. Patwant suffered a heart attack. Recovering from it, he found himself thinking of what would have happened had he been a peasant farmer from one of the poverty-stricken villages near his country house at Ghamroj in Haryana, fifty miles or so from Delhi. Almost certainly he would have died because there would have been no hospital near enough to save him. The thought nagged, and when he was better Patwant went to look at the area more closely. He found the villages poorer than he had thought, the land arid or salinated from bad irrigation; eye diseases caused largely by vitamin deficiency were so prevalent that any child who survived infancy had a 90 per cent chance of eventually suffering from cataracts or glaucoma; survival beyond infancy was reduced as a possibility by the high rate of gastroenteritis; tuberculosis was on the upswing among cattle and therefore human beings; and the women were still in semi-purdah, living withdrawn and repressed lives inaccessible to family planning propaganda, for though these were Jats of Hindu faith, the areas had long been under Moslem domination.

Coming back from his tour, Patwant had an experience that sounds like one of the incidents in the legends of the Buddha's life. From his station wagon he saw a group of peasants by the roadside, obviously in distress. In their midst a young woman lay in agonized labour; she would die if she did not get help quickly. Patwant told the peasants to lift her into the back of the station wagon and told his driver to go straight to the military hospital in Delhi, where he had friends; her life and the child's were saved. The incident seemed like a sign. Patwant decided to create a small hospital so that such a need might never more arise among the peasants of Ghamroj.

He got to work immediately, badgered the state government of Haryana to give him a piece of barren land and recruited his architect friends to design an open campus of small pavilions that he could build cheaply out of fieldstone and other locally available materials. He talked manufacturers into giving him beds and sheets and cement. He recruited retired Sikh army doctors, charmed Delhi specialists into offering their services at nominal cost and persuaded a couple of English nurses travelling in India to stay on and help him set up the hospital and its extension services. Above all, he turned to the vast, international circle of friendships he had built up in the years of pleasure and embarked on great annual pilgrimages to collect funds in Britain, the United States and especially Canada, where he tapped the consciences of lumber-rich Vancouver Indians and persuaded the Canadian International Development Agency that his Kabliji Hospital and Rural Health Centre was a voluntary venture worth supporting.

It was at this stage that Inge and I—old friends astonished at Patwant's transformation—became involved, seeking a way to put the gathering of funds in Canada on a stable basis. With a few doctors and other old India hands, we set up a group called Canada India Village Aid. Behind it was the thought of returning to Gandhi's ideal of village regeneration—long neglected in India and sadly downplayed in Sir Richard Attenborough's film *Gandhi*—and treating Patwant's Kabliji Hospital as a model experiment that might be replicated elsewhere. One of the people attracted to our group was Toni Onley. Watching us working at banquets and book sales and garage sales to draw in money at a time when all charities were complaining of declining donations, he said to me: "You're piddling away your energies for a few dollars. Why don't you and I go to India together? I'll paint, you can write, we'll make a book together and sell the paintings into the bargain."

I agreed, and we planned a trip whose contrasts we felt could show the diversities of India, that continent masquerading as a country. Starting from Delhi, we would go to Rajasthan and then to Fatehpur Sikri and Agra to get the historic India of the Moghuls and Rajputs: palaces and mosques, deserts and castled hills. We'd fly south to Kerala and its lagoons and palm groves and the end of the land at Cape Comorin. From Trivandrum we'd cross the Deccan, by way of Bangalore and Hyderabad, to the great temple complexes of Orissa on the Bay of Bengal. Then, through Calcutta, we'd climb to Darjeeling and the Himalayan vistas and so through Delhi out of India to Burma on our way home. But first we would visit Kabliji.

Ghamroj, where the Kabliji Hospital was built, lay on a secondary road out of Delhi on our way into Rajasthan. It was the kind of hopeless countryside, exhausted by three millennia of cultivation since the Aryans moved down into the Jumna plain, that Inge and I already knew from having wandered around with Gandhian volunteers in 1961. The tired, dusty soil grew crops of stunted maize and sugar cane. The adobe houses in which the peasants lived were so near to literal mud huts that we would often be aware of a village only when we were about to enter it, so closely did these settlements blend into the brown land. The hospital, with its low, hexagonal buildings, fieldstone outside and whitewash within and roofed with lichened tiles from old British bungalows, had the same low-squatting look, and the peasants sitting huddled under their grey-white cloaks on the beds were able to look out at eye level on fields like their own, where teams of oxen limped to and fro dragging wooden plows much like those used by Roman farmers two thousand years ago.

When we got there, the sewers in many villages were already covered and clear, safe water was being drawn up from the rebuilt wells. And we heard, in big, old houses deserted by absentee landlords, the dry-wood clank of handmade looms and the light chatter of knitting machines. We halted in doorways decorated with ancient patterns of molded plaster and lifted our joined hands in the *namaskar* gesture as we waited for the women to garland us with marigolds and dab our brows with auspicious red powder and offer us sweet chunks of *burfi* before we stepped in to see the work that has changed the life of women in these villages. In the open courtyards hung with the bright-patterned dhurries they wove there were women of all ages: teen-age girls at the knitting machines, married women at the looms, old women preparing the yarn for weaving. Within a few months after the looms appeared, the last vestiges of purdah vanished and the women began to assume a more equal role in village life. One result has been the steady rising of the age of marriage, as girls begin to find they have earning powers, from fourteen or fifteen to nineteen or twenty, with a consequent dramatic reduction of the birth rate. Even the status of widows, the traditional pariahs of Indian villages, has improved since the hospital began to employ them as aides and give them a rank in the community.

The effort throughout has been to foster change within the community itself, which is why, instead of sending paramedics into the villages from outside, the Kabliji Hospital has chosen to train the traditional *dais,* or local midwives, in simple hygiene and medicine so that new influences can enter village life through customary channels.

As we drove out of the compound at Kabliji, a cart drawn by white oxen with blue-painted horns was coming in; a man lay in it, wrapped almost to the eyes in a dirt-grey cotton cloth, so that we could not tell his age, but the woman who squatted beside him on the jolting floor of the cart held the fold of her faded green sari over her face, leaving only her eyes visible; she was one of the old school. Whatever was wrong with the man, he had a hope that wouldn't have existed four years ago, before Kabliji was built, when the only recourse was a distant hospital with no ambulance to reach it.

Jaisalmer represented the past—India as it had been. Kabliji looked into the problematical future—India as it might be. In between, along the roads and airways we would follow in the coming weeks, was the changing India of the present with all its political confusions and its obstinate social anachronisms.

Toni Onley and I came at the beginning of our journey to a reasonable understanding of the division of our roles. He is a landscape painter, but he never fills his landscapes with human figures. I am a travel writer deeply concerned with the way people live in the countries where I make my journeys. Our complementary functions were easily defined; I would populate with my prose the landscapes Toni rendered in his evocative watercolours. And so, while I wandered in the towns to observe the people and absorb the flavour and detail of their lives, Toni would be as likely as not to be found outside the city walls, building up with his elusive colour washes the essential structure of land and monument.

When I travel I am given to dawdling and apparent idleness, through which I absorb my impressions by a kind of slow osmosis, and so I was often astonished at Toni's diligence and endurance. He would come back with his legs badly burned because he had sat too long in shorts in the seashore sun of south India, but he would have three or four paintings to show for his sufferings. At Darjeeling, the great comb of Kanchenjunga was visible only in the mornings and best just after dawn; Toni would sally out with the first light to Tiger Hill, where at eight thousand feet on a January morning the ground would be bitterly frozen. The driver would run around gathering sticks on the mountain to make a fire to keep Toni warm enough to function, and newspapers had to be burnt carefully over the completed paintings to dry them out.

Though Toni did not paint people, the irrepressible curiosity of the Indians drew them towards him, and he was rarely lacking an audience. We would draw our boat up to an island in a lagoon near Cochin and, under the arching palm trees with nobody in sight, Toni would start to paint. Within a quarter of an hour, people would appear as if from nowhere—the dark, bright-minded Malayalis, coming by canoe from the other islands, standing on the shore beside us to see this exotic wonder, and every now and again breaking into a chant of "Beautiful!

Beautiful!" If the Malayalis were admiring observers, the implied criticism of Indian bystanders was not always flattering. Once, on the rocky hillside outside Akbar's rose-coloured deserted city of Fatehpur Sikri, an old *sanyassin*, a holy man with tangled hair and ragged orange robe, stood before Toni for a while, watching silently, and then suddenly squatted down and crapped on the rock beside him before disdainfully walking away. But perhaps the most unequivocal tribute was one that nature paid to art. In his last painting of the desert city of Jaisalmer Toni felt he had to break away from the tyranny of the enamel-blue sky, so he painted in a good, heavy gunmetal-grey cloud. The next morning, in that town where it had not rained for four years, we woke to the smell of dampened dust as a shower licked over the battlements and vanished into the desert.

One day at Kovalam on the Malabar coast, when we had been looking at a batch of his watercolours, Toni turned to me and said: "You called your book *Faces of India*. Why don't you call this *Walls of India*?" It fitted the kind of painting he was doing, and I realized that it dramatically reflected my own developing thoughts during those weeks back in India. India, of course, has always been a country of symbolic walls, walls between states whose people speak different languages, walls between religious communities (especially Hindus and Moslems and lately Hindus and Sikhs), walls between castes, walls between classes, always much higher and more visible than the walls that divide more homogenous societies like those of the West.

When I wrote *Faces of India* twenty years ago, I acknowledged that the walls were there, but I believed they would dissolve into more human patterns of interconnection. After all, in 1961 Gandhi had been dead only thirteen years. Nehru and the ruling group in Congress had indeed adopted the direction of Western-style nationalism, stressing military power and industrialism as the solution to India's ills. But a good many people still remembered the incidents at the end of Gandhi's life that have been ruthlessly edited out of Attenborough's recent and lamentably inadequate film: Gandhi's exhortations to Nehru to disband the Congress Party because he "smelt corruption in the air"; his warning that "the militarization of India would mean self-destruction"; his argument that "self-government means the continuous effort to be free of governmental control, whether it is foreign or whether it is national."

Gandhi's alternative to the industrial and military state that Nehru chose to make India was a decentralized confederal society built up from the villages where 80 per cent of Indians then lived, and in 1961 it seemed an ideal not too quixotic to accept, since India was still a fluid society where nothing was finally settled, where the walls appeared to be breaking down, yet where the old world of diverse cultures was still vitally alive and nothing had yet hardened enough to take its place.

Twenty years later, on our way through Rajasthan, I find myself sitting with a former maharajah in the apartment he has been able to hold on to in the great palace his father built; he is a softly handsome, plummy-eyed man who talks nostalgically about his days at Oxford. The talk goes evenly until I mention Attenborough's film, and then I see a glint of Rajput fury suddenly appearing in those soft brown eyes. Did the film somehow malign the native princes, I wonder? Not at all. The loss of his privileges has brought this former prince nearer than one might have expected to his unprivileged former subjects, and he goes into an eloquent tirade about the hypocrisy of the Congress politicians who wear their handwoven garments to pay lip service to the Gandhian image and have forgotten the poor to whom he devoted his life. I do not ask what the maharajah himself is doing for the poor, since I have heard, travelling through the state his ancestors used to govern, how he had given away most of his wealth to prevent it from getting into the hands of the Men of Delhi, as he contemptuously calls them. He refuses even to discuss the Woman of Delhi.

A burst of spite? A bunch of sour grapes? Perhaps. But I'm not sure how relevant that criticism is, since my experience is that those who have in some way wielded power are often the most acute critics of those who now wield it. They know the temptations, and if they criticize their successful rivals for doing what they themselves might have done, that may merely render their perceptions all the more acute.

Power, and the greed for it, were certainly two things I saw in plenty as I travelled over India this past winter and witnessed the great political manoeuvres that overthrew the governments Mrs. Gandhi had sponsored in the two great southern states of Karnataka and Andhra Pradesh. And always, like shadows in the struggle, I saw the Walls.

At first sight, indeed, it seemed as though the Walls had grown less substantial than in the past, for the initial impression of India in the 1980s is one of creeping homogenization. The landless peasants flee to the towns and get submerged in the great bustees, or shack suburbs, that spring up around all the larger cities. The urban culture moves out along the busy trunk roads that stretch like sleazy ribbons of uniformity from one end of the land to the other. And, whatever the language of the region one enters, the wares shown in the shops and stalls have rarely any longer a local look; they come out, shoddy and synthetic, from factories whose products are almost identical whether they are situated in Bombay or Baroda or Bangalore. The special character of local cultures is being leached out everywhere except in the remotest tribal regions, and the consequence is that poverty, which comes better coloured than plain, is deepened by alienation from the inherited lifestyles.

These are perhaps social phenomena, but they cannot be dissociated from the trend towards political centralization that Nehru and his associates took over from the British, in direct contravention of Gandhi's decentralist model for the future India, and that has been greatly speeded along since Indira Gandhi came to power in the middle sixties. After jailing tens of thousands of her opponents during the so-called Emergency, under laws established by British viceroys, Mrs. Gandhi has been busily trying to subordinate all the state governments run by her Congress (I) party to tools of the central government; in Karnataka, one of the reasons she lost the recent elections was that she had forced the resignations of four chief ministers of the state in two years.

Yet behind the appearance of social and political homogenization, the Walls remain, more solid than ever. The sense of community is strong and usually negative in its manifestations, so that earlier this year Assamese Hindu tribesmen have massacred

Moslem Bengalis they regard as intruders, Moslems have burned down parts of Kerala towns in communal riots and Akali Sikhs in the Punjab have been drifting steadily towards the separatist position of the Kalistan movement that only a year ago was treated as an eccentric fringe group financed by a few crazy Vancouver Indian millionaires. Mrs. Gandhi's crushing defeat in the Andhra Pradesh elections was caused by the sudden appearance of a new party dedicated to the preservation of Telugu culture and dominated by Rama Rao, the former leading star in Telugu films; Tamil Nadu to the south is already firmly in the hands of another regionalist party led by the leading Tamil film star.

More sinister and growing taller than the solid Walls created by religious and linguistic differences are those created by caste. Twenty years ago everybody in India thought that caste was on its way out. In the 1980s it has assumed a new and evil importance in the hands of politicians. Castes were originally occupational groups that were later given religious sanction and a ranking system. These aspects of caste have become blurred over the years, but the basic institution is as strong as ever, since caste groups have re-emerged as voting blocs, manipulated by but also manipulating the politicians. One of the most striking aspects of the recent state elections was the way both the forecasts and the post-mortems of the political commentators were dominated by calculations of the strength of various candidates in terms of the caste group they could call upon. The struggle of caste has moved beyond mere electoral action into group violence, and during the six weeks we were in India a series of killings took place at two universities—Patna and Baroda—arising out of struggles between student caste organizations. All this has meant a virtual end to ideological politics in India; even the Communists in their strongholds of Kerala and Bengal have to play the caste game to get the votes.

And then there is the great enduring Wall that divides India even more dramatically than Disraeli's England into two nations—the Privileged and the People. Everywhere one is told—except by people in power—that "the rich are getting richer and the poor poorer." I am unaware of any body of statistics that could give one a bearing by which to follow this question through the economic situation of India's 700 million people. But the self-evident fact is a vast mass of poverty that seems irreducible in any foreseeable future. Indian social commentators seem agreed that at least 300 million (more than one-third the present population and equal to two-thirds the population at independence) are at the lowest level of subsistence, with no land, no housing better than shacks, no jobs worth the name, no prospects. One sees them every day along the roads of India. The only road machines in use are diesel rollers that press down the stones laboriously chipped by hand and put into place by hordes of people—mostly women and children—who work for less than $1 a day and in some remote areas for as little as 50 cents.

At the bottom of this great pile of destitution there are sensational areas of exploitation that remind one of the revelations of Engels and Mayhew about the worst of early nineteenth-century Europe. A recent scandal about children being killed by explosions while making fireworks revealed that in one small area of southern India there were 45,000 children younger than fifteen working in match and fireworks factories; the youngest, aged between four and seven, were being paid two rupees (less than 25 cents) for a twelve-hour day and were virtually indentured by parents who could not afford to do without their earnings. At the same time, another scandal broke around the notorious brothel district in Bombay known as the Cages, which horrified me when I saw it twenty years ago and apparently has not changed: 10,000 prostitutes, many of them kidnapped children, were being bought and sold by madams at prices between 5000 and 7500 rupees—$600 to $900 a body. India, it turns out, has the highest population of working children in the world, more than 16 million of them between five and fifteen, wretchedly paid and often working under dreadful conditions. One of the mainstays of the Kashmir carpet industry is a corps of 7000 child victims of asthma and tuberculosis between the ages of eight and ten.

There is no lower level to which this mass of the Indian poor can sink. Yet on the other side of the Wall there is a growing middle class, and the everlasting Indian contrast between the rich and the poor is emphasized by the conspicuous spending of this new class, which shares the callousness and vulgarity that in every time and place are characteristics of the nouveau riche. Again, statistics of the size and wealth of this class are hard to come by, since tax evasion is rife in India and few people reveal their real incomes, but it seems likely that about 100 million people (one in seven of the population) have benefited in some appreciable way from the growth of industry and commerce and the development of mechanized farming in a few favoured areas such as the Punjab. The best-off among these people fill the kind of hotels that in the past catered to well-heeled tourists and inhabit the big, new suburbs of expensive and tasteless villas that have appeared on the outskirts of the large cities, offering dramatic contrasts to the crowded and insanitary bustees where many of the workers live in close vicinity.

But perhaps the greatest Wall of all walls is that created in Delhi—that agglomeration of the ruined and standing walls of nine successive cities—between the rulers' symbolic conception of India and the reality experienced by the people. This was dramatically demonstrated by the Asian games held there last year. According to the estimate of Patwant Singh's magazine, *Design*, a total of approximately $500 million was spent from public and private sources on building stadiums, athletes' villages, overpasses, roads and a mass of new hotels; some of the hotels were not finished in time for the games, and those that were completed were not filled because the expected international crowds did not arrive. This occasion brought no benefit to India except a little prestige among the nonaligned countries, but it consumed vast amounts of money on a nonproductive venture in a year during which several thousand people died of famine in Bihar, bustee dwellers near the sites of the games had still to make do with one water tap for one hundred or more shacks and literally hundreds of millions of Indians had neither pure water nor enough to eat.

And yet, and yet... there was the Kabliji Hospital and a dozen positive ventures like it that we encountered on our way, scattered dots of light perhaps, but....

At the end of our trip I reread *Midnight's Children* and understood better its strange mix of vigour and nihilism, of obsession and rejection. I detected the symptoms of falling out of love and remaining attached that I myself was undergoing. For whatever I have said, I knew I would return, hoping against hope, when I stood on our last morning in Darjeeling and watched the mists drifting up the steep hillsides among the splendid decrepit mansions towards the deodar-crested ridges and the clouds shredding away in the distance to reveal the glistening splendour of Kanchenjunga.

It is not for nothing that India has a great compelling two-natured goddess, black Kali and brilliant Parvati, horror and beauty in one.

Back to Spain

1986

WHEN WE WENT back to Spain, we avoided the coastal highway from France that leads to the crowded beaches of the Costa Brava. Instead, we turned inland to the old French walled city of Carcassonne and went on towards the Pyrenees through the arid valleys of La Corbière, where meagre vineyards grow a harsh and pungent wine. On the hilltops stood the ruins of castles where, in the twelfth century, troubadours sang to lords and ladies in the courts of heretic noblemen known as Cathars. The Cathars believed that the material world was evil and that Satan was a god coeval with Jehovah and just as powerful. In the thirteenth century, Pope Innocent III declared a crusade against the inoffensive Cathars; their castles were besieged and the inhabitants burned in grisly mass bonfires. In these bleak grey valleys, under a lowering autumn sky, it was easy to believe that an aura of tragedy from that terrible past still hung over the landscape. I think we were all relieved when, at a little spa town called Aix-les-Thermes, the road began to climb in great loops through the chestnut forests into the mountains.

We, I should say at this point, means the painter Toni Onley and his wife, Yukiko, as well as Inge, my wife, and me. Toni and I had travelled in India two years before, gathering the material out of which we made our book *The Walls of India*. Now, once again, I was introducing him to territory he had neither painted nor even seen before—Austria and Bavaria, the mountains of the Bernese Oberland, southern France and Spain. Inge and I had been to Spain twice before, once in the late 1960s and once in the early 1970s, and each time we had liked the country and the people. As we left Carcassonne I remembered and quoted a remark by Marcel Proust, the gist of which was that it is always unwise to go back to places where one has been happy. But none of us took it seriously.

Our way across the Pyrenees took us through the tiny country of Andorra, high on the mountain divide between France and Spain. The pass rose 2400 metres into the clouds, out of which a little frontier post loomed; an Andorran in a green uniform waved us into his 465-square-kilometre country. Then the road levelled. As it tipped south towards Spain, we drove suddenly out of the mists and the sun shone brightly on the tan-coloured mountain pastures and the first ski hotels of Andorra.

It seemed a good omen, but in the end Proust turned out to be right. Even Andorra was not what I had remembered. Only a generation ago it was a Spartan little mountain community whose precarious independence was guaranteed by the joint suzerains, the president of France and the bishop of Urgel in Spain. Traditionally, Andorrans had lived by rearing cattle and sheep on the high pastures of the Pyrenees and by smuggling, for which their position on the French-Spanish frontier gave them splendid opportunities. By the time I first reached Andorra in the 1950s, it was in the early stages of transition from smugglers' realm to tourists' paradise, and there was a naive charm to its commercialism. Resplendently dressed porters would stand in the roadside outside the scattered new hotels trying to wave in the few cars that arrived over the narrow dirt road from France. Now, the winding valley bottom that forms Andorra's only artery had become a long ribbon development with hotels, custom-free emporia, banks and jewellers' shops jostling each other and the cars of the newly rich Andorrans taking up most of the parking space. I thought at first that the hotel porters were still functioning, but then realized I was seeing the

Andorran police directing the heavy traffic in their new theatrical uniforms of purple jackets and bright blue trousers. It has all become very much like a tourist town anywhere in Europe, a little more plebeian than Davos but just as crowded, and it took some ingenuity that night to find a rustic restaurant of the kind we remembered. But eventually we succeeded—it was probably the last of its kind—and I had for dinner a large bowl of small upland snails in a sauce of pungent mountain herbs, followed by roast pork with baked aubergines and a selection of Pyrenean cheeses, with a good tart rosé wine from Navarre.

In the next two weeks, as we went south through Aragon towards Toledo and then into Andalusia and the western border regions, we realized that Spain had changed in ways about which neither the Michelin guide I carried nor its Baedeker rival had given us any idea. Most countries are changing so quickly, and the changes so affect travellers, that we need a new kind of guidebook that will still tell of the ancient sites and the famous art works but will also prepare people for the kinds of problems and difficulties they may now encounter in finding them.

The people who use guidebooks are not the trippers who merely want two weeks on a sunlit beach or who are willing to follow their guides obediently on a conducted tour. They are the people whom I call the genuine travellers, because for them the journey is as important as the destination. They make their own arrangements. They travel in their own or in hired cars on the same roads as the people of the country; their experiences are largely determined by the luck of the road, the unplanned encounters, the small places to which chance leads them on their way to famous sites, the side roads they happen upon and the inns to which by fortune the end of a day's journey brings them. Such travellers enter with varying degrees of intimacy and insight into the life of the country they traverse. Their experiences are conditioned by all kinds of social circumstances of which the Costa Brava sunbather and the client of Dinky-tours are mostly unaware. They are the people most in need of up-to-date information on what to expect when they try to find their way through a strange country, and they are therefore the most likely to be disappointed by the way the writers of guidebooks evade uncomfortable reality.

The reality of Spain, for example, is that in the mid-1980s it is undergoing revolutionary changes in three directions: a belated industrial revolution, a rapid population shift from the country to the cities and a growing annual flood of tourists that has now reached 40 million. All these affect the foreign visitor and condition his enjoyment of the country.

In a land that survived until recently by exporting its agricultural products and by allowing foreign companies to exploit its mineral assets, factories with inadequate pollution controls are now appearing everywhere and creating miniature Sudburys where once there were quiet market towns. The increase in industry also makes travel less comfortable. This, in fact, was the only point where my Michelin guide gave a slight hint of what we might expect. "Spain suffers from poor communications," it said. "Roads remain, in spite of improvements, uneven and congested as most commercial traffic travels by road." That is, at best, an understatement. The Spanish railway system is still astonishingly primitive and is largely taken up by military traffic; we saw several trains of tanks and guns travelling on flatbeds through the countryside, visible signs of the power the army retains despite the wide democratic reforms of recent years. The greater part of industrial and agricultural transport uses a highway system constricted by the many mountain ranges, so one can rarely escape onto the kinds of deserted side roads in which the French countryside abounds. Mostly, as we edged from place to place during our two weeks in Spain, we found ourselves caught in long snakes of traffic whose pace was determined by ill-maintained trucks belching clouds of black diesel fumes, so that by the time we went back over the Pyrenees, all of us were suffering from minor respiratory troubles.

At least Michelin hints at difficulties on the road, but it does nothing to prepare travellers for the effects of Spain's rapid urbanization. Rural areas I remember to have been well populated fifteen years ago are now inhabited mainly by old people. Farming has been largely mechanized, the young have fled into the towns in search of employment and the urban areas have grown in what to the outsider looks like unplanned confusion. Now one approaches old cities where mediaeval walls and church towers not long ago stood out as landmarks in a wide open countryside and finds one's way barred by besieging rings of factories, warehouses and raw, new utilitarian apartment blocks set in vistas of rubble and garbage.

One of the parts of Spain I most enjoyed on earlier visits was the distant province of Extremadura on the Portuguese frontier. Even in the early 1970s it was still a rustic countryside given to breeding pigs that fed on the acorns of the cork oaks, to grazing sheep whose cheese is widely eaten, and here and there in the valleys to growing a little wheat and tobacco. It was the kind of harsh region that all through history had exported its most vigorous men. Pizarro and the other conquerors of Peru in the sixteenth century almost all came from small towns in Extremadura, like Trujillo and Cáceres, and when they returned from the Indies as rich conquistadors, they turned these towns into fine cities by building great mansions of gold-coloured stone. The contrast between the frugal living of the present and the wealth the region once briefly enjoyed gave its special flavour to Extremaduran life.

In the last few years there has been great progress in Extremadura, and its effects have been all the more striking because the region until recently was so primitive and so conservative. The valleys are being irrigated, and new crops like cotton are being grown. Local industries have appeared. There has been an obvious rise in the standard of living, and the once ubiquitous poor peasant with his overburdened donkey—the prototype of Sancho Panza—has become a rarity, though mechanization has up to now been unable to replace the shepherds, who still wander over the countryside raising great clouds of dust as their mingled flocks of sheep and goats graze the autumn stubble.

The effect of all this rapid change has been to submerge the fine old towns of the region in such a surge of construction that at first sight they are virtually unrecognizable to anyone who visited them a few years before. Mérida is an example—an ancient place where many buildings constructed by the Romans

2000 years ago are still standing. When one entered Mérida in past years, the view was dominated by the tall arches of the aqueduct that brought the water into the Roman city. This time I had to look hard before I saw those elegant arches, dwarfed among a cluster of jerry-built apartment blocks. There had been no attempt to fit the ancient and the new together in a planned environment.

Mérida is no exception. Ancient and beautiful cities throughout Spain are suffering the same thoughtless and unsupervised expansion. One of the great sights of Spain used to be the splendid eleventh-century walls of Avila, which stands on a plateau over 1300 metres above sea level. "The walls are complete," says Michelin. "They dominate the landscape from afar." Alas, the guidebook is no longer accurate; a new town is arising outside the walls, and the tide of building has already blotted out what was once the most dramatic view of the city—from the west, seen as one drove in over the mountain pass.

Of course, there are still small places in Spain that have somehow been preserved in all their old character, and there are still sites whose breathtaking beauty has not been spoiled. As we wandered over the great dry plateau of La Mancha, through kilometres of vineyards crowded with autumn pickers, the image of Don Quixote came poignantly into our minds as we reached the little white community of Consuegro. We saw the long line of windmills, still intact on its castled hill as it had been in the days when Cervantes invented the Knight of the Sorrowful Countenance. There are still few views of the Spanish mountains as starkly magnificent as the one we enjoyed for the couple of days we stayed in the *parador* at the Castillo Santa Catalina in Jaén on the way south to Granada. And we were back in a Spain we recognized with delight when we went westwards out of Granada to Arcos de la Frontera on suddenly empty country roads, through dazzlingly white little Andalucian towns like Olvera and Algodonales, filled with bright flowers and each dominated by its castle of golden stone and its massive baroque church.

Arcos is one of the most beautifully set towns in Spain—a tangle of ancient alleys, steep narrow streets and old whitewashed buildings, built on a high spur of rock where there is no space for the jerrybuilders to get a foothold. The town square is right on top of the rock, surrounded by the castle battlements, the richly carved church of Santa Maria and the big eighteenth-century House of the Corregidor, which has been turned into a parador.

Having mentioned them twice, I should say something about paradors, the places where we mostly stayed in Spain. They are state hotels, the best and often the only accommodation in rural areas, usually located in converted old buildings, often of historic interest, such as castles, convents and mansions. A decade ago they were unbelievably inexpensive, usually between $6 and $8 a night for a double room. Now they are priced in the same range as ordinary hotels, from $45 a night in smaller places to $70 in centres like Toledo and Granada, where they are getting run-down from overuse. But they offer what is often excellent value, and the parador at Arcos is still exceptionally well run, with one of the best restaurants we chanced on during this visit to Spain. For dinner—eaten late in the Spanish manner (round about 9:00 P.M.)—we had cauliflower cooked in a bed of leeks; a dish of perfectly grilled, small red mullet with tiny, crisply fried potatoes from the olive groves; a kind of almond custard with fried sweet pastries; side dishes of black pudding, piquant sausage and large olives marinated with local herbs, and a tall earthenware crock of local red wine from the Jerez region, pungent and full. Such meals have become exceptional treats in Spain today. In most restaurants the tendency is towards food cooked heavily in oil—those 410,000 tonnes the groves produce every year have to be used up somehow—and the service is far more peremptory than it was in the leisurely, *mañana*-dominated past.

But for me—and this is the main reason I go back to Arcos—the great attraction of the parador there is the high and precipitous cliff on whose edge it stands, with the rapids of the Guadalete River glistening far below. The cliff is inhabited by great colonies of birds: jackdaws and silvery-grey pigeons and elegant little pink-and-grey falcons. To sit taking one's drink on the terrace of an evening as the sun falls reddening through the

Back to Spain

dust haze towards Jerez and the river below turns into a silvery mirror catching the last of the sky's light, and to watch the aerial gradations of these birds who live in such miraculous harmony, is to me one of the great experiences of Spain. Up to now it has been an unspoiled experience.

Almost alone among the larger cities of Spain that we entered on this visit, Toledo has avoided the fate of being overwhelmed by its own growth. It too has grown, but intelligent planners seem for once to have taken control, and instead of chaotic suburbs crowding the access to the old city, industrial and residential areas have been built in the hills some kilometres away and well out of sight. The original Toledo, with its cathedral and its churches and its ancient walls, still clusters on the hill around which the river Ebro runs like a moat, spanned by bridges built by Arab kings 1000 years ago. As Toni Onley recognized when he made his own luminous watercolours of the place, the cityscape has changed very little since Domenikos Theotokopoulos, the man whom the Toledans called El Greco, painted it four centuries ago.

I never did find out why Toledo made so much more graceful an entry into the modern world than other cities, for my time was taken up by one of those misadventures about which Michelin had not warned me. Inge and I had gone down from our parador, which stands on a hilltop about three kilometres away facing the city. Parking our car by the river, we found our way to the cathedral, past the brutal block of the Alcazar and through the narrow streets, many of them now malls, with their shops selling such Toledan specialties as marzipan and damascened swords.

Like the cathedrals in most major Spanish towns, that in Toledo is a jumble of architectural gems under a single great roof—chapels and choirs, a chapter house, a treasury, a sacristy—in a variety of styles from Moresque through Gothic to baroque. There are marvellous things to be seen there, like the great fourteenth-century retable of gold-leafed larch wood in the sanctuary, recording in carved detail the life of Christ, and the gigantic gold monstrance in the treasury—three metres high and made by a sixteenth-century German master—that is paraded through the streets of Toledo at Corpus Christi.

But in the cathedral, as elsewhere in Toledo, it is the ethereal vision of El Greco that predominates. The church of Santo Tomé has his most famous painting, *The Burial of Count Orgaz,* but in the sacristy of the cathedral there is another equally important work, *El Espolio,* of the disrobing of Christ before the crucifixion, as well as a series of El Greco's imaginary portraits of the apostles.

I was especially interested in *El Espolio,* because the painting had caught the eye of Canadian poet Earle Birney and had led him to write a remarkable poem about the carpenter in the foreground of the picture, who is going about his work of making the cross, ignoring the indignities that other figures in the background are wreaking on a fellow carpenter, Christ.

We left the sanctuary and were walking back to the main door, discussing the painting and arguing a little, for Inge preferred El Greco's portraits and I considered *El Espolio* one of the greatest paintings I had seen, when I was tapped on the arm.

A neat little man stood there, dressed in the pale blue shirt and grey trousers that seemed a summer uniform among Spanish clerks; he had a camera around his neck and carried a little tote bag; his companion, garbed in the same respectable way, stood beside him. "Look, señor," he said in a plummy Madrid accent. "Your jacket!" And indeed, streaked down the back of my coat was what looked like an ample bird's blessing. The little men came forward solicitously, opening their tote bags and pulling out tissues, which they offered us. I took off my jacket, and Inge put her handbag on a little step at her feet where we could both see it and started to clean the coat as best she could. We wiped off much of the mess, and the little men walked off, to turn a moment later and point excitedly to the roof. "Look!" they shouted. "The pigeons!" We looked, seeing no pigeons, and when we looked back Inge's bag was gone. In the instant our attention was diverted, some accomplice we never saw had slipped by and lifted it. By now the little men had vanished, and it was hopeless to hunt them down in the maze of chapels and entrances.

Our anger at the loss, and our sense of shame as old travellers who had thought themselves immune from such mishaps, were mingled with an appreciation of the professional skill the thieves had shown. It was a well-crafted job, and as a craftsman of another kind I admired it. Meanwhile we had to salvage our situation as best we could. We went first to a cathedral guard. He was uninterested; his job was to protect the churchly treasures, not the purses of foreigners. We would find a policeman outside. We did, in charge of a large van, but he refused to do anything because he had to look after the vehicle. We must report at the police station. He gave us elaborate directions on how to find it in the maze of little streets. When we did reach it, we were told it had been closed for reconstruction and that we must go to the great police barracks three kilometres out of town where, eventually, we made our report through an interpreter and looked fruitlessly through great volumes of mug shots. Nothing came of it, of course; indeed, we got no real help from official Spain. The clerks of Air Iberia, the only airline with a local office, refused pointblank to get in touch with KLM on our behalf to replace our stolen plane tickets, and the sole genuine co-operation we had was from American Express in Madrid, which arranged quickly to issue new travellers' cheques at the next large town on our road.

The developments in Spain I have been describing in this article—the spread of industry, the crowded roads, the great suburban sprawls—all are features of the process by which an old and backward society emerges rather awkwardly into the modern world. They are balanced by a rise in living standards that seems astonishing when one reads of the terrible poverty of rural Spain during the 1930s in books like Gerald Brenan's *The Spanish Labyrinth*. Spain is still a poor country compared with Switzerland, but there is now one car for every five people, and peasants who once lived in hovels lit by oil wicks now have modern apartments. Such changes are inevitable and beneficial, even if they have been poorly planned, and the traveller, who is only a guest, must adapt to them and find his way to the old and the historic through the chaos of the new. My quarrel with guidebook writers is that they will resolutely concentrate on the ancient treasures at the heart of a modern city and tell the traveller nothing of the maze he must follow to reach them.

They also say little about local attitudes towards strangers and the way they may change. For a quarter of a century now, Spain has been deluged with tourists; at last count the number of foreigners entering the country each year exceeded the number of resident Spaniards. Inevitably this has affected the way visitors are viewed. When Inge and I first went to Spain in the late 1960s and the early 1970s, the rule of General Franco was slackening, and there was a general air of expectation over what would happen when the old dictator died, as he must do very soon. People from the outside world were welcomed with all the traditional Spanish courtesies, partly because they were still relatively few and partly because they represented a world of freedom that the Spaniards looked forward to rejoining.

Spain rejoined that world of freedom almost a decade ago. Its people now know the problems as well as the privileges of democratic life; the visitor from the outside no longer brings with him the promise of a better world. At the same time, catering to the tourist has become a major factor in the Spanish economy; as Michelin reports in an unusual wry moment, tourism "is to twentieth-century Spain what Peru was to the kingdom in the sixteenth century." But familiarity has bred, if not contempt, at best indifference and at worst resentment, so that the stranger does not encounter the same helpfulness and courtesy he encountered a decade ago. Even if there were no tourists, Spain is moving out of its ancient feudal modes, and the old courtesies are disappearing even among Spaniards. They are becoming modern, preoccupied, urban people like the rest of us.

What else would I say in my ideal guidebook? I would warn the traveller that the newfound prosperity of Spain is not universal. Particularly in the south there is still much poverty, and the recent world recession has aggravated it. In Granada you can, of course, have a charmed day or two on the great hill over which the Moorish palaces and the oriental gardens of the Alhambra and the Generalife are spread out. It is a little more crowded with parties of German and Japanese tourists than in the past, but in the quiet enclave of the Parador San Francisco or in one of the old Victorian hotels on the hillside, one can still live like a heroine in a Henry James novel, out of touch with life's real harshness.

But go down into the noisy city and the gasoline fumes of the Calle Reyes Cataloicos, and the picture changes. We walked one day through the narrow lanes behind the cathedral and took a lunchtime snack at one of the tables outside a bar in the Plaza de la Trinidad, where the flower sellers and wreathmakers have their stalls. It is not a tourist haunt; most of the customers are young Spanish working women. But in about forty minutes we were approached by no less than twelve people trying to get a little money from us. Two women, one pregnant and one with a small child, begged openly and quarrelled bitterly at our table. An old man tried to sell wind-up flamenco dolls, and a deaf mute came with a card explaining his predicament. Four young men were shoeblacks and looked with annoyance at our suede shoes and sandals, and four more were trying to sell small packets of Kleenex. The Spanish workers gave to the beggars and the deaf mute, and we followed suit; Spain has yet to develop a welfare system like ours, and many of the poor are helped only by random charity. As for the nine people trying to sell things, I doubt if during the forty minutes they made $2 among them on our corner of the plaza. To watch them taught one a lot about the marginality of young people's lives in Spain today. But there were other mordant lessons as we wandered farther into the heart of Granada: old decrepit men in the ruins of good business suits, selling lottery tickets or begging, and the most agonizing sight of all—a young couple, reasonably well dressed, intelligent looking, with a glint of privation in their eyes, kneeling together on a busy pavement, holding up a banner saying they had long been out of work, their children were starving, and they asked not for gifts but for justice. All the pride and despair that so often surge up together in Spanish history seemed personified in that desolate couple, and I walked on troubled that I could not somehow give them the justice they demanded. The willingness to accept such encounters and respond with feeling distinguishes the traveller who wants to understand a country from the mere tripper, and the good guidebook, it seems to me, should prepare him for them.

Finally, a good guidebook on Spain should warn about thieves in sacred places, like those we encountered in Toledo, but should also note that robbers come in many guises. Motorists should keep their eyes particularly open for the predators of that notorious rural police force, the Guardia Civil, who set up traps on the highroads frequented by tourists to catch them committing technical offences. This happened to us on the road near Burgos. Toni was driving up a long gentle hill, with a broken median line, when the truck driver in front signalled him to overtake. He and a French driver did so; as the two cars overtook the truck, the line changed from broken to solid, and there the jackbooted Guardia were waiting. They charged each driver $100; there was no way of evading payment, for they arrogantly impounded drivers' licences and car papers until the "fines" were paid in cash.

How much found its way into official coffers we had no way to know.

So, if you go to Spain according to my guidebook, drive circumspectly, distrust strangers in churches, keep small change for the poor, who are often needy if not always deserving, remember always that you are guests in a society in the process of rapid and racking change and, above all, do not be put off by a city in the throes of expansion; there are usually jewels in the heart of the rubble.

The Caves in the Desert

1987

THERE WAS A garrulous Kiwi on the train from Beijing to Datong in the province of Shansi. He was going much farther, into the desolate borderlands of Sinkiang, where he worked as a seismologist creating artificial vibrations to gauge the presence of oil deposits under the Chinese deserts. His only English-speaking companion for the next month would be the taciturn Australian who worked with him in an otherwise all-Chinese gang. He was eager to get in as much conversation as he could while there were people around who spoke his language. He kept coming back, standing in the doorway of the compartment with his fuzzy black beard and his blue cap advertising a Manila beer, grousing about the interference of Communist Party officials in complicated technical problems.

As he talked, the train puffed its black coal smoke over the plain beyond Beijing, where the fields were green with winter wheat, and through low mountain ranges, where whole valleys were white with wild plum blossom and we saw fragments of the Great Wall running over hill and dale, and on into Shansi, over a yellow plateau of arid earth dotted with herds of tiny sheep and the ruins of the watchtowers that had once given warning of the Huns invading from the north.

Socialist democracy demands that there should be no first- and second-class compartments on a Chinese train. Face is saved by providing a "hard" class for most people and a "soft" class, more comfortable and also more expensive, for the minority. The comfort consisted of cushioned seats covered with well-washed canvas and decorated with antimacassars, which are ubiquitous in China. The conveniences we did appreciate were the gigantic thermos flask, holding about five litres, and the set of lidded teacups. The six hours of our journey were punctuated by the appearance every hour or so of a pink-cheeked teen-aged girl in a blue uniform, carrying an immense iron kettle with a canvas cosy, from which she would replenish our thermos. The food in the dining car, as we had been warned, looked too dreadful to be worth experiment, so we drank tea and ate biscuits and bananas we had bought in the little shops outside Beijing railway station. And as we sipped and nibbled, Ziyi, the amiable young official from the Ministry of Culture who accompanied us on our whole journey and made most of the arrangements, told us romantic stories about the watchtowers.

An emperor had a beautiful wife with whom he was in love but who never smiled. One day she asked what would happen if the beacon fires were lit on the watchtowers. Anxious to please her, he ordered that the torch be put to the fires, and the nobles came out with their military levies and paraded before the emperor and his queen, expecting a Hun invasion. But the Huns did not come, and the lady laughed uproariously. A month later there was a real alarm. The fires were lit, but this time the nobles thought it was another hoax and did not call their men together. The Huns invaded and the kingdom fell. For the first time, as I heard the story, I began to realize how nostalgic Chinese have become in the late 1980s, almost forty years after the successful revolution, for the romantic past that the Cultural Revolution so violently rejected only a few years before.

We left the lonely seismologist at Datong. We did not realize that, except for a couple of days in Xi'an, we would not be seeing many more Caucasian faces than he did. For we had marked out an itinerary whose three principal destinations were ancient

The Caves in the Desert

sites not on the usual tour routes. Two of them, the Buddhist sanctuary of Wutai San in the depths of the Shansi mountains, and the vast complex of ancient painted caves at the oasis of Dun Huang on the edge of the Gobi Desert, had only recently been opened to foreigners, and in any case are not easy to reach. The first of the three, which was Datong, had up to now been preserved from an excess of travellers by the lack of an airport. But ten kilometres away from the city was one of the great Chinese monuments, the sacred grottoes at Yungang, with their gigantic Buddhas carved fourteen centuries ago.

Datong itself is an ancient place turning modern, with chunks of tamped-earth city wall left over from the Ming dynasty, wide imperial avenues, an old town of narrow streets where the great tiled roofs of ancient temples tower over rows of low shops, and in the middle distance the chimneys and surface works of the big state-owned mines, for this is coal country.

Outside the station a small smiling man in sports jacket and grey flannels stood beside a Toyota van; this was Meng, the head of the local cultural bureau, and the van would provide our transport for the days we travelled through the Shansi mountains, to and beyond Wutai San. Apart from Meng and Lan, the driver, our party consisted of Paul and Xisa Huang, our friends who run the Bau-Xi Gallery in Vancouver, their eleven-year-old son Liang, Ziyi from the Ministry of Culture and, of course, my wife and me.

The next day we set off for Yungang, past the big collieries and into a countryside broken by little valleys and gulches. There I had my first introduction to the pluralist economy of China, for coal around Datong lies in surface outcrops as well as in deep seams, and little mines were burrowing into every slope; the road was full of beaten-up trucks and scurrying tractor trailers taking the coal into the city, where it would be peddled around the houses and into the villages for sale to the peasants. All these mines were run by individuals or by small partnerships, who paid a royalty to the state and kept the rest of the money they earned. It was an extension into another industry of the changes in farming by which the great communes of Mao's day were abolished, and the peasants began to till their own strips of land for their own profit. Judging by the number and activity of the people involved, the pluralist system seemed to be working as well in mining as in farming.

But the Yungang caves belonged to a different age and a different world. During the fourth and fifth centuries —a millennium and a half ago—there had been a great upsurge in Chinese Buddhism. It was the time when Fa'Hien, a Buddhist monk, went on his famous journey through the Gobi Desert to India to obtain the sacred Sanskrit books of the religion, which he translated into Chinese; Fa'Hien's successful return after fifteen years of wandering gave a great stimulus to the faith, to which the emperors of the reigning Wei dynasty were devoted. Work was started on the caves at Yungang and at the same time at Dun Huang, far to the west, the other end of our journey. The two places were united by the Silk Road, along which not only merchants but also religious teachers (Nestorian Christians and Manicheans and Jews, as well as Buddhists) found their way into China. They brought with them not only theologies but also art styles, particularly the hybrid Greco-Indian style from Gandhara, near the Khyber Pass, where the earliest Buddhist sculptures were made. Gradually this hybrid style became naturalized in China and changed into an authentic, native art.

Construction on the Yungang caves began in 460 under the patronage of Emperor Wen Cheng, who sent a monk named Tan Yao to organize the work. Tan Yao assembled brotherhoods of lay volunteers, artists and craftsmen and began the great assault on the kilometre-long stretch of sandstone cliff that we saw far down the road as we approached the site. Seventy caves, large and small, were eventually hacked out in a period of about a century, and 50,000 sculptures were made—figures of buddhas and bodhisattvas and devis and arhats and other sacred beings, cut from the rock in high or low relief. The largest were giant sculptures ten or twelve times the height of a man; the smallest were tiny buddhas only as tall as a thumb, carved in such numbers and with such repetition that sometimes they would diaper the whole wall of a cave.

We approached the caves through gardens and paved courtyards dotted with pavilions holding massive bronze bells, and

The Caves in the Desert

small worship halls turned into restrooms and souvenir shops, all crowned with the deep curved roofs and dark crusts of tiles in which the Ming dynasty excelled; all were much newer than the sculptures in the cliffs. A sound unfamiliar in China immediately caught our ears: the chirping of sparrows, which had become almost extinct during the great bird extermination campaigns carried on in China during the 1950s to the detriment of the country's ecology. In the old sacred places they seemed to have found refuge, and at Yungang they shared it with the sand martins that had built in the cliffs and soared constantly over our heads.

My immediate impression of the Yungang caves was that of an eroded version of the great temple of Karnak in Egypt, for the first set of grottoes—the last to be carved—is protected by an arcade whose tall, massive and irregular columns were hacked out of the rock. In some of these later, more elaborate caves, the walls and ceilings were entirely carved with religious scenes or with almost abstract patterns based on some holy motif such as the lotus. They had often a fluid lushness that was rather un-Chinese and reminded one that Buddhist art, like Buddhist religion, came originally from India. In one of the largest caves a complete and intricate pagoda soared up into the darkness, carved out of the living rock. The cave beside it had been scooped out into a dome like the inside of a miniature St. Peter's, the sides decorated with turquoise paintings of buddhas and the ceiling with devis flying in elaborate circles, so that the impression was one of flames swirling around the head of the great Buddha, nineteen metres high, who sat under the dome with a dwarf disciple, the mere height of an ordinary man, standing on his gigantic thigh.

Beyond the colonnade stretched the early caves cut out by monk Tan Yao and his helpers 1500 years ago; the great Buddhas, seated in the lotus position, and the Maitreyas (future buddhas), seated western-style on thrones, were carved out of the cliff-face. Once they had been protected by wooden roofs (the sockets for the beams could still be seen), but now they stood open to the sun and sky, and though their colours had vanished, they were surprisingly undamaged and crisp in outline—too solid for the weather to destroy, too massive for the Red Guards to mutilate. The largest of them was twenty-three metres high (almost eighty feet), and in his massive presence, looking into the ironic calm of his gigantic face, I felt dwarfed mentally as well as physically, rather like Gulliver with the king of Brobdingnag. It was not merely the sheer size of the image; it was not even the sense of being present at a great moment of artistic transition, embodied in the contrast between the statue's Chinese features and its Greek-style draperies. It was, rather, the same kind of awe I had felt in the presence of a great collective faith—in the Gothic splendour, for instance, of French mediaeval cathedrals such as Chartres and Bourges.

Naturally, I wondered about the feelings of the Chinese who came here; the visitors were all Chinese except for us and one stray Australian girl. I talked to a group of young people in pale blue uniforms who wanted to practise their English on me. They were trainees for counter jobs on the state airline, sent out from Beijing on a cultural tour as part of their training, and their attitudes varied from bored indifference to curiosity to a pride in their country's past. Other people were more actively repossessing their cultural traditions, sitting in the sand on the cave floors to capture in brush and ink the details of the statues. And some had come to pay honour, to bow before the Buddha and to offer joss sticks and biscuits shaped like half moons and gifts of money—even though this was not an active religious centre as were some of the places we later visited, and there were no monks in attendance as there were in the old Huayan temple in the heart of Datong.

The sense of tradition renewed was intensified that evening when we went to the first of many opera performances we attended on our journey. It was the local Jing opera, in which the basic story is not cluttered with acrobatics and other diversions, as is the case in Beijing opera. I had expected at least some vestiges of the highly propagandist style encouraged during the Cultural Revolution, when militant operas such as *Red Lantern* and *Taking Tiger Mountain by Strategy* were in vogue. But there were no revolutionary songs, no choruses in the uniforms of the People's Army strutting across the stage with rifles and red

The Caves in the Desert

flags. It was as if the clock of theatre had been put back a whole generation.

The opera was a tale of aristocrats in love during the T'ang dynasty, and the audience of miners in their blue working clothes and market women in their little white sanitary caps listened enrapt as the plangent voices of the elaborately gowned and coiffed and jewelled singers unfolded the tragic history. The art of engagement had come to an end; we were seeing the art of escape into a romanticized past.

We witnessed this returning to the past in quite different ways as we took our mountain journey from Datong to Wutai San. It was a long day's travel through bleak ranges and over plateaus of yellow loess, in which the villages, built of mud the same colour as the soil, seemed concealed in the landscape. Some villages, in fact, consisted of walled-off caves like those outside Granada in Spain. In other ways, I was reminded of the Andes, since even the steep slopes were terraced into little fields that must have been worked with spades, for there was no way a tractor or even one of the little mule-drawn wooden plows of the region could have been driven up to them.

In a cleft in the mountains we came to an architectural curiosity called the Hanging Temple. It was a lonely sanctuary that straggled over the cliff-face into which it had been ingeniously cantilevered so that it seemed to hang like a cluster of swallows' nests. It had been built fourteen centuries ago and often repaired, but the original principles of anti-earthquake construction had been maintained. When we first saw the temple, we thought it was supported on a series of tall pillars lodged in the rocks below. But when we clambered up the narrow stairways, among the May Day holiday makers from the nearest village, to the straggling galleries of the temple, we realized that these timbers merely hung down loosely, and it was only when the building was under strain that they actually settled down into their sockets and supported it. This was the only temple we saw in China that was dedicated to all three traditional religions: Buddhism, Confucianism and Taoism. The statues of the founders of these cults were exhibited together in one room, and while the Buddha retained his serenity, both Confucius and

Lao Tzu, the founder of Taoism, were represented as scowling blackly. They had never agreed when they lived and knew each other 2500 years ago, since Confucius was a law-and-order philosopher and Lao Tzu a primeval anarchist, and the statue makers had gone to pains to project their incompatibility.

Over more mountains and valleys we came to a little town called Ying Xian, in which all that was left of a once-great temple was the oldest and largest wooden pagoda in the world. The Wooden Tower stood almost seventy metres high and had survived weather and earthquakes for nine hundred years. Preserved in the dry northern climate, it was still a remarkably sturdy building, with its six roofs supported on ancient elaborate bracketing, its rooms full of grave wooden statues and Sung murals of ferocious Heavenly Kings, its bronze bells ringing sweetly from the multiple eaves, and the swifts soaring high in the air around it.

The village council insisted on offering an impromptu feast in our honour, and I sat with Meng and Lan and some of the local cadres as the cooks got to work and we talked about rural superstitions. Everyone agreed they were returning in strength after the attempts to stamp them out during the Cultural Revolution. The astrologers, in particular, were back at work. And arranged marriages are in fashion again among the peasants, and this means not only that both sides have to build good houses out of profits from the free market, but that horoscopes have to be exchanged to make sure the families can propitiously unite. I had a feeling, talking to the Party men, that they had given up resisting the return to the past. "The peasants want it," one of them said, and in the special mystique of Chinese communism the peasants have always been the important class, as Mao Zedong taught; after all, in spite of urbanization, the inhabitants of China's 700,000 villages still make up three-quarters of the country's population. When students rebel, the government and the Party can brush it aside as the flicker of a butterfly's wing compared with the inertia of a billion people. But when the peasants reclaim their way of life, as they have done increasingly in recent years, it is as if a dragon were awakening, and the snorts of fire from his nostrils have to be watched cautiously.

The Caves in the Desert

All these anxious matters were forgotten when the cooks were ready, and we settled down to an interminable ceremonial meal of thirteen or fourteen dishes, most of them too rustic to be familiar to a Canadian connoisseur of Chinese food. The *tour de force* was a large dish called Son and Mother—stewed chicken topped with deep-fried hard-boiled eggs, washed down with excellent local beer and followed by a long series of bottoms-up toasts in fiery rice liquor, during which the name of Norman Bethune, the only Canadian of whom most Chinese had heard, was heavily invoked.

Celebrations in Ying Xian delayed us so much that when we reached the deepest core of the mountains and began to climb the high pass towards Wutai San the sky had darkened and snow had begun to turn the rare villages into grey and white checkerboards. The road rose, narrowed and became slippery. At 3000 metres we topped the pass and began to descend slowly into the deep cold valley of Wutai San. By this time the light was going, and the low-slanting rays were hitting a cluster of temple roofs, minute in the distance, on a snow-covered peak to the east. We descended among buildings that were becoming shadowy presences, a great hall looming here, a stupa probing the pale sky there, until we were in the bottom of the valley and driving up to the new hotel a local co-operative had just opened.

It was a good hotel, built by workmen from the area whose families had preserved the crafts of temple building from generation to generation. It had massive tiled roofs, large comfortable rooms and good food, with a leaning towards Buddhist vegetarian dishes. The only other guests were Chinese, some from Hong Kong.

It's time I said something about Chinese hotels. Bad hotels, of course, are one of a travel writer's staples. Like most of my kind, I have enlivened the tale of many a dull city with a Dickensian description of the horrors of its hostelries, and before I reached China I expected opportunities of this type.

After all, we had been led to believe that one could expect good hotels only in places where foreign visitors congregate, such as Beijing, Xi'an, Shanghai, Guilin. Elsewhere, it has been said for years, the hotels are inferior, and this was supposed to be one of the reasons why the Chinese tried to restrict the scope of travel.

Perhaps this *was* true; it is so no longer. New hotels are being built and old ones refurbished at such a rate that even a recent and commendably adventurous guidebook like *China: A Travel Survival Kit,* published in 1984, is quite out of date both in its description of the current facilities in the various cities and in its judgement of existing hotels. Only once in our month of travel did we come to an inn whose deficiencies were dramatic, and that—to which I shall refer in due course—was in a place where even Chinese travellers rarely came. Two hotels, one of them in Beijing, were hideous neoclassical structures, built in the period of Sino-Russian friendship and visibly decaying. But in many places, where foreign visitors must still be numbered in the dozens rather than the thousands, we found new, efficient and comfortable hotels. I liked the fact that the Chinese have not been infected by the mania for hard beds that has swept the hostelries of western Europe and North America. One could usually rely on a comfortable medium-soft bed with a good cotton-stuffed quilt to keep one warm. As for the food, western breakfasts were served in most places but were usually wretched, and I chose the Chinese breakfasts of gruel, steamed buns, pickles and sweet cakes when I could get them. In the hotels where we stayed, the main meals were always Chinese, lunch and dinner both of ten to fourteen courses and offering local specialties which most people, if their expectations were not set in the Cantonese cuisine naturalized in Canada, would find interesting and palatable.

Daylight at Wutai San revealed the amazing splendours of a community which, since the T'ang dynasty in the eighth century, had been one of the four great pilgrimage centres of China, dedicated to Manjusri, the sword-bearing Bodhisattva of wisdom. The People's Army used it as an easily defensible guerrilla stronghold in their campaigns against both the Japanese and the Kuomintang. But the temples survived, and today there are said to be fifty-seven of them, although I did not make a count and suspect that the total includes many small shrines. I had expected to find a dying place interesting only for its past, to walk

The Caves in the Desert

through ravaged gardens to ruined buildings. I found a living sanctuary that was symptomatic of China's present-day way of life.

With their elaborately timbered and heavily tiled roofs supported on massive wooden columns, the temples stood on hilltops, from which deep stairways cascaded into the valley. Tall pagodas and stupas celebrated the great saints and scholars of the past. The halls of the temples stood in flagged courtyards dotted with bronze incense burners and miniature pagodas and stone sundials. Vermilion-stuccoed walls defining the temple properties clambered over the hillsides. The first almonds were blossoming in shrill pink, and fresh green needles were beginning to show on the larch trees. As environmental architecture it was all superb, as fine as anything in Japan. The Chinese, of course, contend the Japanese are mere imitators.

The temples had not only survived; they were open and active. There was a large community of monks in grey and brown robes, and sometimes in the maroon robes of lamaist temple members. They were not merely old men from China's past; more than three hundred novices lived in the temples, studying and chanting the sutras before the altars. Among the pilgrims, women and old men were doing a brisk trade in Buddhist rosaries, which spoke well for the freedom of both commerce and religion.

Few of the people were sightseers. It was too cold and too early for that. The visitors had come to pay their respects to the great presences, to the towering bronze or painted stucco statues of Sakyamuni and Manjusri and Maitreya. A company of monks of all ages, wearing sheepskin jackets under their red robes, had come from a remote abbey in Inner Mongolia, and a group of wild-haired herdsmen had accompanied them. Climbing up one of the staircases we met three gigantic monks from Tibet, and when we greeted them in Tibetan they replied in the broad accent of Kham, the land of warriors and brigands.

But most of the pilgrims were Han Chinese, and they were of all ages. Frail old people struggled up the tall steps, supported by staffs, to ring the five-tonne bronze bells and paste on them scraps of paper with prayers for the living and the dead. Middle-aged women walked the lanes muttering mantras as they counted off the 108 beads of their rosaries. There were also young people making their offerings; I saw one man of about thirty in a blue Mao-style suit teaching his young children to kneel on the cushions and prostrate themselves to the great gilded impassive images as they spoke their prayers.

In the South Temple the abbot invited us into his parlour. A tall, wispy-bearded old man in a burnt-orange brocade robe, he gave us green tea and Danish butter cookies which a Hong Kong pilgrim had brought as an offering. He was wearing a hearing aid patched up with surgical tape, and he told how when the Red Guards came to Wutai San he had been forced to kowtow, had been dragged on the ground and beaten so badly over the head that he lost his hearing. But now he and his fellow monks were left in peace. They even received a small pension from the government, and with what they grew in their gardens they could keep going. I had a feeling that most of all he was grateful for survival. Another abbot had been killed.

A few days later we were in Lanzhou, the capital of Gansu, the long arid corridor of a province through which the Silk Road ran between Mongolia and Tibet towards the Gobi Desert. We had left the cold valley of Wutai San and travelled south through the central Chinese countryside, searching out village temples, visiting cities such as Taiyuan and tiny mediaeval towns like Pingyao where we ran into Donald Sutherland and Phil Borsos making their film on Bethune. We had then gone to the tourist centre of Xi'an, mainly because it was the hub of air routes from which we had to get to Lanzhou and northwestern China. We did not neglect the area's archaeological sites, however: the fascinating neolithic village of Banpo, the great processional way lined with T'ang statues at the royal tombs of Qianling and Xi'an's over-famous pottery soldiers. But Dun Huang in the Gobi Desert was our third main destination, and Lanzhou, a bizarre industrial town that straggled thinly for seventy kilometres along the Yellow River, was our jumping-off point.

At Lanzhou I had a birthday, and the local cultural officials gave a party to celebrate it: a little banquet with suckling pig, and a desert dish of lamb cooked in chafing dishes at the table, and squid stew, and baby eels, and many dishes of noodles and vegetables and exotic fungi, and the year's first tart lichees, with frequent toasts in sweet heady peach wine and in a fiery rice liquor called Happy Li Po, which was chosen to honour me as a writer. Li Po was a great Chinese poet; according to legend, he drowned drunk in the Yellow River trying to embrace the reflection of the moon. During the desultory conversation over the poet's drink, we mentioned Wutai San and its pilgrims to a man whose garb and manner marked him as a good party cadre. Of course, he assured us, religion was free everywhere in China. Why, there were nine hundred Catholic churches now open and active!

"But surely Marx taught that religion is the opium of the people," said one of us. Our party man was unperturbed. "Of course, that was only Marx's opinion," he lightly replied, and then went on to talk about the difficulty he himself found in writing poetry when he held such a taxing bureaucratic post. I was left marvelling. For it seemed to me that a crucial stage had been reached when the words of the prophet could be dismissed as an opinion.

In Lanzhou we had a setback, which turned out to be fortunate. There was a sandstorm in the Gobi Desert, and an exceptional shower had turned it into what was called "yellow rain," so that planes could not fly to Dun Huang. The head of the local cultural bureau suggested that we go by road instead—up the Silk Road. He ordered out the department's minibus, and early the next morning we set out on two long days of hard travel covering the 1200 kilometres between Lanzhou and Dun Huang.

The old caravans had long disappeared from the Silk Road, and its sand tracks had been replaced by one of those rough roads the Chinese still make by hand labour. Camel trains had come this way until the 1930s, and the mud ruins of the caravanserais still stood at intervals of about twenty kilometres, the distance of a night journey by camel or wagon; in those days it took at least two months to cover what we travelled in two days. It was desert country most of the way through the Hexi corridor—golden sand dunes or flat expanses of dark pebbles dotted with tamarisk bushes. The brightly tinted volcanic ridges of the Longshou Shan ran to the north of the road, and Mongolia was over its crest, thirty kilometres away; to the south the great snowy Qilian Shan rose more than 5000 metres (18,000 feet), shielding the borderlands of outer Tibet.

The Great Wall was our almost constant companion, running for many kilometres beside the road, and here it was not the trim, restored masonry that one sees near Beijing, but the mud wall originally built at the order of the Han emperors 2000 years ago to protect the Silk Road. It had weathered according to the strength of the prevailing winds, and sometimes there were long stretches of wall seven or eight metres high and four thick, with the watchtowers and gate towers standing massive and clay yellow over the bleak wasteland. The only settlements were widely spaced oases, though once we passed a great cluster of crumbling ruins where three hundred years ago an emperor had been led by a dream to order that a city be built in an uninhabitable desert. Often we were alone with the wall, and I remembered poignantly the sad old Chinese poems about the desolate exile of military service on this forlorn frontier.

We passed through no more than four towns in the whole 1200 kilometres, and these I recognized as ancient trading centres on the Silk Road. Wuwei had then been Liangchow, and in one of the many generals' tombs found there the famous bronze flying horse was discovered. Zhangye was the Chang-ye where the great pilgrim Fa'Hien spent the winter of 400 A.D. on his long way to India. In the old hotel there they gave us sacks of rice for pillows, and the newly installed bathroom was ankle deep in water for lack of plumbers. But in the back streets of that ancient town we found an old temple with an immense and beautiful reclining Buddha, and stored away behind it a collection of bronze life-sized statues, the newest a thousand years old, which had been collected in abandoned desert temples and were totally unknown outside Zhangye.

But such things fell temporarily out of memory—though they were safely lodged in my diary—when we crossed a last desert, white with saltpetre, into the great oasis of Dun Huang

The Caves in the Desert

and saw the Magao Caves, which are often called the Caves of the Thousand Buddhas.

You leave the oasis and travel farther into the Gobi to reach them. A narrow valley with a trickle of water allows a cool grove of desert poplar and flowering elm to grow, and behind it rears up a tall cliff of conglomerate rock that holds back the spectacular dunes known as the Singing Sands. There are about a thousand caves cut into the cliff. Those to the east are unembellished burrows where the old monks live. To the west are the five hundred painted caves.

Most visitors—and there are still not many—are whisked through quickly by the guides and shown perhaps a dozen caves. We were lucky enough to gain the confidence of one of the curators—the excellent Mr. Ma—because of some special knowledge about the western end of the Silk Road in Afghanistan and Iran that I was able to pass on, as one enthusiast to another, and so we saw more than fifty caves, and those were the best.

The first caves at Dun Huang were carved out and painted in the fourth century A.D. and the last during the Yuan dynasty in the fourteenth century. During this thousand years Dun Huang was not merely a religious centre where hundreds of monks gathered to live the religious life on the edge of the desert. It had another and more worldly aspect, for it was a great junction point of the Silk Road. The main highway—if one can apply that title to tracks in the shifting sand—ran west from China towards Turkestan and Afghanistan and Persia and eventually Europe, and the highway that crossed it ran northwards from Tibet into Mongolia. Dun Huang, the junction point, was also the place where the merchants and their caravans took on supplies and did their best in other ways to ensure good fortune before they started on the terrible stage across the Taklamakan Desert that begins just west of Dun Huang, and over which it was said that one found one's way by following the bones of men and of animals. Offerings were made to the Buddha, and rich merchants or officials would often pay for the decoration of a cave and for the construction of statues. The rock at Dun Huang, which consists of pebbles held together by clay, did not lend itself to sculpture, as the sandstone at the Yungang caves had done. The Dun Huang statues were all made from armatures consisting of bundles of sticks or canes bound together with linen thread, over which the bodies would be molded in mud, and then a fine surface layer of stucco would be added and, finally, they would be painted. The paints used were pure mineral tints obtained from caves in the volcanic mountains across the valley and mixed with sheep's tallow; the technique was really a primitive kind of oil painting.

The desert, with its average yearly rainfall of nineteen millimetres, gave the ideal climate for the preservation of these works. The great destroyer was the sand that blew into the caves, which were square structures like the inside of a Chinese house, with pyramidal ceilings and fairly narrow entranceways. The entrances would suffer, and also the altars that faced whatever wind and light came in. And this had some very interesting results. Taken as a whole the caves represent a remarkable anthology of Chinese and central Asian Buddhist art. The paintings in the earlier caves are often distinctly Indian in character, with broad-waisted, heavy-breasted female deities. Often, also, there are Persian influences. Then, about the seventh century, Chinese styles appear, first the T'ang and then the Sung. But often, as perhaps was inevitable in a centre where so many artists congregated over so long a period, there are signs of experimental urges: the bold dramatic outlines of expressionism, elaborate patterns that turn a lotus blossom into an abstraction. Since the caves had been maintained over so many centuries, there were often extraordinary combinations of styles. A cave would be made in the Sui or T'ang dynasty, and the frescoes in the inner chamber would remain as they were originally painted, with colours often of pristine brilliance. But the sand would have made it necessary to repaint the entrance hall, and so the friezes of lady and gentleman donors would be portraits done—often with great irony and eloquence—in the marvellously expressive line of the Sung painters. The figures on the altars would sometimes have been blurred by the blasting sand—or possibly defaced by one of the Moslem invaders who sometimes rode into Dun Huang—and then one would find that some rustic crafts-

The Caves in the Desert

man had imposed an expressionless pudding face in white stucco on a splendid molded body with the eloquent draperies at which the T'ang sculptors excelled.

Apart from the artistic interests, the caves were a mine of marvellous documentation, a veritable pictorial history of mediaeval China. There were great processions of traders on the Silk Road making their way around the four sides of a cave in all their variety: man and animal, armies on the move with archaic armour and marvellous banners, scenes of village and palace life worked into ancient Buddhist stories. It was a vast anthology of custom and folklore and history, as well as a museum, left in situ, of a thousand years of Asian art. I do not think I have ever seen, in forty years of exotic travel, a single site so rich in interest as Dun Huang.

During the early twentieth century, after being forgotten for ages, Dun Huang was discovered by European archaeologists, notably the famous Anglo-Hungarian explorer of central Asia, Sir Aurel Stein. Unfortunately, Stein arrived just after an old Taoist priest living near the caves had discovered a bricked-up grotto full of rare manuscripts and other documents, including the world's first known printed books. The most recent of them was eight hundred years old. In those days archaeologists tended to be scholarly predators, intent on gathering specimens for European or North American museums, and Stein—like Franz Boas in British Columbia—was in this respect no better than the rest. He persuaded Wang, the Taoist priest, to sell him the best of the documents and shipped twenty-nine packing cases of them to the British Museum, where they have been stored away in the cellars for seventy years and more. French, American and Japanese scholars followed to claim their share of the loot, and the result is that the little museum at Dun Huang, where it should have remained, has only a tiny remnant of this vast and wonderful library. But fortunately, only one statue was ever taken away from the caves, by a covetous American collector, and the Gobi Desert was too far off for the Red Guard to do much damage there.

Apart from the oxidization of some of the colours, and the bad restorations I have mentioned, the caves at Dun Huang are still in relatively good shape and are now protected by louvered iron doors, which the Ministry of Culture has prudently installed. There is even, in the oasis of Dun Huang, a respectable hotel.

We returned through Lanzhou and Xi'an, siphoned that way by the air routes, and then went south into the areas of southern China around Guangzhou, which seemed a different country from that we had just left, for here it was all green fields and water, whereas we had come from sand dunes and the dry beds of vanished rivers; here the ancient wooden temples, which the dry air preserved in the north, had long decayed and vanished. But in social terms it was not much different. In the south, as in the north, there was the bustle of the new pluralist China, and perhaps the image that best fits them both is one I carry in my mind from a town roughly halfway between the two regions—an image of one of the free markets of China.

It took place close to our hotel, and we were able to observe it at intervals throughout the day, from six in the morning, when it began, to five in the afternoon, when it came to an end. The city had provided rough plastic roofing over the sidewalks on each side of the streets, but the vendors sold from their own stalls or vehicles. The market extended for a kilometre on both sides of one street and for half a kilometre on each side on a cross street, making in all four kilometres of vendors quite closely packed together. Allowing about 2.5 metres per vendor, there must have been over 1500 people selling at any one time. But, particularly in the vegetable section, where the peasants from outside the town sold from their own tricycle trailers, there was a steady turnover of sellers, some leaving when their loads were sold and others moving in, so that probably during the day there were at least 2500 private vendors in this one market; there were several others in the city.

Every kind of food was sold: vegetables, fruit, meat, fish, bean curd, spices, noodles, rice, oil, eggs (including delicacies like quails' eggs), cakes and bread, nuts; there were goldfish and books, furniture and fabrics, shoes and clothing, trinkets and toys. As well as a vast variety of perishable goods, almost everything sold in the state-run department stores was being sold here by private traders, and usually more cheaply. From morning to night the buyers came in a steady stream. Consumers were satisfied, peasants and craftsmen and peddlers were making money for themselves, people were finding employment, and the traditional Chinese love of trading and trafficking was being satisfied. The people who travelled the Silk Road for 2000 years would have felt at home here. I make no political comment.

My Worst Journeys

1989

MY IDEA OF a worst journey is conditioned by the fact that long ago, in my boyhood, I read a book on Robert Falcon Scott's antarctic expedition, which came to a tragic end only a few days before I was born in 1912. The book, by Apsley Cherry-Garrard, was called *The Worst Journey in the World,* and even now, when I think of bad journeys, that title echoes in my mind. In an absolute sense, a worst journey is one that ends, like Scott's or like Vitus Bering's voyage to Alaska, in death. We admire the fortitude with which such men endured their cumulative hardships and the kind of grim resignation projected in the last sentences of Scott's diary: "We shall stick it out to the end, but we are getting weaker, of course, and the end cannot be far. It seems a pity but I do not think I can write any more." This was after Scott and his companions had learned that their efforts had been in vain, that Roald Amundsen had reached the Pole before them. Adding to their sense of failure was the growing certainty that exhaustion, starvation and the bitter weather were making it impossible for them to survive long enough to return to their base camp. Behind the stiffest of British upper lips, fear must have been there, and a growing sense of the futility of heroism.

Physically and mentally, in its progress and its results, Scott's was a "worst" journey in an absolute sense. For those of us who have survived our travels, there are only worse journeys; for our experiences, on this side of dying along the way, are relative, not absolute. But that at least allows one to make comparisons.

In deciding which is the worst of worse journeys, there are many criteria to be considered, and when I think of them, each draws out of my memory different incidents. Am I thinking of extreme physical discomfort? A bone-racking bus journey in the Mexican highlands comes to mind, with a maimed driver who negotiated dangerous corners by controlling the wheel with the stump of his right arm while crossing himself with the fingers of his left. And there was a painful shoreward walk over sharp coral and tin cans—always watchful for deadly stonefish—when a copra boat landed me thigh-deep in a South Sea lagoon. But far more vivid are my memories of one night in the early 1950s, at a place called Monterrey, at the centre of the Callejon de Huaylas in the Peruvian Andes.

Monterrey had been a parody of a European spa until the publicity about its "radioactive" springs suddenly began to scare away rather than attract the hypochondriacs who used to come up from Lima to stay for a week or so of sparkling waters. The neglected baths were now green with weed. The hotel was dingy. The food was heavy in the Peruvian way: many dirty courses served each night at about ten.

I was already suffering from the mountain sickness locally called *soroche*—a bit incoherent, prone to faint in the dining room. And then, in the middle of the night, my wife, Inge, and I were both seized by violent attacks of dysentery. At the same time, the electricity and water supplies failed simultaneously, and no servants answered our plaintive calls for candles when we ventured into the dark corridors. So, attacked by spasms, we would make our stumbling ways to the bathroom, where we would become nauseated once again by the rising stench, until we would fall back exhausted on the bed. But even then, weary as we were, we could not sleep even fitfully, for it was the night of an Indian festival, which was probably where all the servants had gone. From farmsteads near the hotel came the beat of drums and harps, the shrilling of quenas, the high-pitched chant of women singing Quechua songs. We looked out from our wretched darkness and saw the people round their fires in what at that moment seemed to us an obscene and mocking sabbath.

The night passed. In the morning the water came on again, and we staggered down, exhausted, to get on an early bus for the next stage of our mountain journey. I was too comatose to be alarmed when the bus was stopped along the road by a squad of the jackbooted and spurred Guardia Civil, who were then the terror of the altiplano. They pushed the Indians off the bus, poking into their bundles and roughing them up with a cruel impersonality that did not arouse a yelp of protest from their opaque-eyed victims.

Then they ordered me into their office, a granite guardhouse by the roadside. "Do not let him go alone, señora," a man behind us whispered, and so Inge and I went together. Perhaps the indifference resulting from our fatigue disarmed the two epauletted figures who sat behind a large desk as we entered, with vast leather-bound books before them. All at once, they became officers and gentlemen instead of tyrants of the countryside, offering us seats, plying us with coffee and accepting cigarettes as they laboriously entered the details of our passports and the intent of our journey into their great registers. My appearance of dignified sang-froid, due entirely to weariness, was spoilt when I had to ask the sergeant in attendance to show me the smeared and stinking latrine at the back of the post. He was a ferocious-looking giant with Hohenzollern moustaches and a sword whose loosely slung scabbard clinked over the stones as he walked beside me. In less urgent need, I might have been scared of him.

We were let go in the end, got back on the bus with the maltreated Indians and dozed almost the whole time until we reached the town where we meant to stay the next night. The sun was just setting; and as we walked up to the hotel door, I saw another member of the Guardia Civil, also heavily moustached, stepping out from under the shadow of a great eucalyptus to have a look at us. Our movements had obviously been monitored by telephone. But by now whatever one took in those days to slow down one's bowels was beginning to work, the altitude was lower, and we could laugh at our adventure. A bad bit of journey, but not the worst.

There is a special kind of ambivalence to journeys in which one's own discomfort seems mitigated by an awareness of the much greater misery of people around one—though that mitigation adds another dimension of discomfort: the mental spasm of guilt.

I first experienced this on a journey I made in the early 1930s, when I was about twenty. It was the height of the Depression in England, and I was, relatively speaking, one of the fortunate ones, cliffhanging onto a wretchedly paid job in London. But I was earning sufficient money to do a little more than merely survive: I could spare enough to buy the occasional sixpenny Penguin; to see Charles Laughton in *Cherry Orchard* and Laurence Olivier in *Hamlet* at the Old Vic, for fivepence, and occasionally to treat a girl to ravioli at Poggioli's on Charlotte Street, for ninepence. I did not have to undergo the humiliation of those who for years had been living on a near-starvation dole, subject to the weekly insolence of the petty bureaucrats who administered such grudging largesse.

I had a Welsh aunt in a small Glamorgan town who offered me free holidays. One day, when I was visiting her, I decided to take a bus and go to the Rhondda area, the heart of the South Wales mining district. Rhondda has a special place in the thoughts of those with Welsh connections, for one of the finest of all Welsh songs—stunning when the daios from the valleys mass sing it at a rugby match—is called *Cwm Rhondda,* the hill of Rhondda. There are actually two valleys: Rhondda Mawr, the Great Rhondda or the main valley, and Rhondda Fach, the lesser valley or Little Rhondda that branches off from it. I planned to go up Rhondda Mawr, cross over the intervening hills and come down into Rhondda Fach, from which I would make my way back to Bridgend, where I was staying.

It was the worst of times in Rhondda, though it probably looked just a little better than the best of times, since most of the mines were not working, and the smoke that would normally have given a dark, satanic aspect to the landscape was less evident than in more prosperous days. There were even a few green bushes and some pallid grass. Still, it was dismal enough —a long ribbon of a main road with no real gap in the houses, so that it seemed like a single serpentine town, thickening out at each village centre like knots on a string.

The houses were mostly built of grey stone, long turned black from soot. In the middle distance reared the gaunt towers and immense wheels of the pitheads and the truncated pyramids of the slag heaps. Many of the shops had gone out of business, for the mines had slowed down years ago and the General Strike of 1929—disastrous for the workers—had delivered the coup de grâce to the local economy. The people were shabby and resentful. Groups of ragged men squatted on their haunches, as miners do, and played pitch-and-toss with buttons; they had no halfpennies to venture. A man came strolling down the street, dejectedly whistling "The Red Flag" in slow time, as though it were a dirge.

The people of Rhondda had double reason for resentment. In those days, before Welsh nationalism became fashionable, they clung to their language as the last vestige of their identity as a people, sang it splendidly and despised the Anglicized Welsh people of the towns, who mocked them in turn. They believed, rightly, that they had been made to pay more heavily than anyone else for the difficulties of the coal industry at that period; and the fact that English interests controlled the mines increased their ethnic resentment. Significantly, the two areas in Britain where the Communists—entirely in their role of extreme radical rebels—always gained large votes were Rhondda, where Welsh feeling was combined with extreme poverty, and Clydebank, where extreme poverty was combined with ancient Scottish grievances against the English. So it was not surprising that though there was not a soldier or a policeman in sight, I had the uneasy feeling, without being menaced in any physical way, that I was in occupied territory as I walked up the long street of Rhondda Mawr.

I came to the blunt end of the valley, went into a cut-price shop to buy a bag of broken chocolate as cheap insurance against hunger, and took a lane that led towards the hills. The lane soon became a path up a gulch with a few dejected alders. Then I was on the bare, pathless hillside, and as I climbed higher, with a few small inquisitive mountain sheep my only companions, I walked over a moorland where the peat had accumulated for millennia—it was as soft and springy and easy to walk on as the tundra of the Canadian Arctic. Streams had cut deep trenches down to the gravel, and to cross them I would scramble down and up eight-foot banks of what looked like chocolate sponge cake.

But these gullies offered no shelter when a storm suddenly burst over the mountain, a driving downpour that drenched me in a minute, for I had no raincoat. There was nothing for me to do but stumble on, finding the gullies more difficult to cross as the water began to rush down in brown spates into which I slipped, several times, up to my knees. At last, I came to the slope leading down into Rhondda Fach, and the rain ceased.

I was a sad, sodden object, my clothes heavy with water, the chill of the mountainside hitting through the wet tweed as I limped down into the valley beside a slag heap, where fifty or so men and women were industriously picking over the ground. I caught up with a man walking along the overgrown road from the mine into the village, whose damp slate roofs I could see glistening about half a mile ahead. He was pushing a rusty old bicycle that had no saddle and no tires but which served to transport the dirty gunny sack he had tied to the handlebars. He had been picking coal from the slag heap.

"No bigger nor walnuts, man," he explained. The bigger coal had been taken years ago, so long it was since work had been seen in the village. I asked him how long he had been unemployed. "*Ach y fi*, man, it's nine years I've been wasting and wasted." Yet he was friendly, perhaps because I looked such a wretched object that he saw me as an equal in misery. He apologetically remarked that these days nobody had a fire in the village except to cook the midday dinner, if there was anything to cook, so I'd find it difficult to dry my clothes. Then he suddenly brightened. "Try the Bracchi shop, man. They'll have a fire, sure to goodness. And there's glad they'll be for a couple of pence to dry your clothes."

Long ago, an Italian named Bracchi had found his way into one of the Welsh mining valleys and had established a modest café. Others had followed him, but his name had clung, and Italian cafés in the Rhondda Fach were generically called Bracchi shops. The Bracchi shop in Rhondda Fach was a melancholy place, its front in need of paint, a sheet of old cardboard filling the broken part of the window in which stood a few dummy packets of tea and biscuits coated in dust. A dejected girl came from the back. Her black hair and olive complexion were Mediterranean, but her voice had a lilt of Wales. She looked at me with hostility when I talked about a fire, and I think it was because I was humiliating her into admitting that they, too, lit the fire only at mealtimes. Nobody came to buy meals any more. So I spent my tuppence on a cup of tea, which she languidly made on a Primus stove. She thawed a little as the kettle warmed up, and talked of longing to go to London. I hope she got there.

My clothes dried stiffly on me as I travelled back on various buses. I had a shilling left, and at a town where I changed lines, I went into a pub and spent it on grog to warm me up, and took no harm from my drenching. It was a bad journey and a sad one, and whenever people talk of the Depression, the image of Rhondda Fach—its wet slate roofs and the workless man and the Italian girl with a Welsh accent—come into my mind. But it was not the worst of my worse journeys; after all, I could have slipped and drowned in one of the flooding streams on the mountain; I could have caught pneumonia, which in those days was still a killing sickness.

Such journeys, combining one's own physical discomfort with a close view of the misery of others, haunt the memory and come back often. There was another, even more harrowing, in Bangladesh, then East Pakistan. Inge and I ended up in Chittagong, which immediately seemed to me the most wretched, most hopeless town I had ever seen—*rectum mundi,* as I then described it. In the "best" and only possible hotel, where the officers from the freighters stayed and drank themselves sodden from boredom, the "luxury suite" had a "bathroom" that was really a section of balcony where one squatted to shit in a hole and showered under a pipe jutting from the wall, with only a four-foot screen to give a scanty privacy. The nets over the beds were full of holes, through which the mosquitoes flew at will. The palms were drying in the gardens and the fountain in the courtyard was dry and filled with rubbish.

Around it, the beggars clustered—not in ones or twos, but in families and tribes, many of them with limbs deformed and faces partly eaten away by leprosy and other sicknesses. Occasionally, the hotel manager—a Eurasian who talked pathetically of England as "home," though he had never been there—would dart out and urge his bearers to drive them away. "A scandal! In front of a first-class hotel!" he would shout, and rush in to telephone the police. The police never came, and the beggars drifted back, stumbling in one's way, plucking one's clothes, speaking in professional whines. They were everywhere in Chittagong; one was free of them only when driving in a taxi through the lanes of mud-stained hovels. They were dejected, hopeless beggars, without the energy to be aggressive; in any case, that would have been pointless, for there were far too many of them for the supply of visitors, and I wondered how they clung to the edge of survival.

Our own wretched hotel life, being kept awake by the mosquitoes, eating tasteless and suspect food, hating everything we saw and heard and smelt, was in local terms the height of privileged comfort, even though it resembled in no way what we had expected from the posters in Dacca, showing the palm-fringed beaches of Chittagong. "Beaches? What is this about beaches?" the hotel manager had asked; the nearest thing we saw to them were the sand banks that the muddy river deposited as it flowed out to the Bay of Bengal. We flew out eventually via Calcutta to Bangkok, where the modest standards of the Thais looked, in comparison, like those of rich men.

Chittagong is high among my bad journeys, but since I survived and came nowhere near to death, and ended up with the bonus of that curious moral satisfaction that comes when one's own discomfort makes one see more clearly into the misery of others, it was not the worst of worse journeys. The element missing, I think, was fear. Well-founded fear, which takes one through the valley of the shadow of death without abandoning one there, is what makes the worst of worse journeys; the situation is made all the more intense when the fear is somehow mingled with delight.

So, in the hierarchy of my worse journeys, I would place at the summit a trip we made in 1972 to Apolima, the smallest of the islands of Western Samoa. It was a historic island, a kind of natural fortress formed from the peak of an ancient volcano, broken down on one side to allow a little harbour to form in the crater. At one period, a high Samoan chief had held out there for a decade when the rest of the chain was occupied by Tongans and had eventually sailed out to defeat and drive them away. The name Apolima meant "held in the palm of your hand," and indeed it did look like a hand held with the palm flat and the fingers raised. Since Apolima is a very traditional island, we had to go there accompanied by a man of high chiefly status, a school inspector named Afamasaga. We travelled in a beat-up old whale boat with an outboard motor, chugging across the lagoon of the main island of Upolu and through the reef into the open sea, which in the morning had a steady, manageable swell. The cone of Apolima came into sight, and we circled round until we were facing the great natural amphitheatre of the standing walls of the crater, their grey crags and combs half submerged under the surging tropical vegetation.

Another kind of surge soon preoccupied us, for the reef at Apolima was an unusual and very dangerous one. It was not a coral reef, but the actual broken-down and sea-worn lava wall of the crater; and it was entered through a narrow, L-shaped passage between the great rock slabs where, only a week before, Afamasaga told us, the boat carrying the island's new teacher had been swamped, and though he was saved with difficulty, his books had been lost. By now the swell had grown higher, and it was sweeping in tall, green waves over the grey rock and returning in a seething white race. At first, we could distinguish no break at all in the reef, until Afamasaga pointed to an area where the flow, though no less powerful, seemed at least less white and broken.

The boat moved into position. "They always wait for the

seventh wave," Afamasaga said, as the boat tossed and the crew shifted into their posts. One crewman clambered into the bow and stood poised with a pole in his hand. Another climbed onto the awning and sat watching the water, with his hands dangling on each side so that the steersman in the stern could see them. The man in the bow made a gesture, the engine sprang into life, and suddenly we were moving full speed with the blue-green wave towards the gap, and in a few seconds were between the dark rock masses that loomed in the tumbling water. The passage ahead seemed hardly wider than the boat. The man on the awning gestured frantically, left hand and then right hand. We wavered slightly, and then we were in the passage, forging ahead and curving as we went, with the poleman fending off the rock on the port side as we swung round through the L-shaped kink and out with the last rush of the wave into the bay—into the calm water, and the sudden release of quick fear.

I looked at Afamasaga. He laughed softly. "Only men from Apolima can do that. Now you see why it was a great fortress. No Tongan boat ever sailed into this harbour."

Once we were in the calm waters, an idyll of charm and calculation was enacted. A tall, powerfully built Polynesian stood on the beach to welcome us in a tartan shirt and a flowered lava-lava. He was the second chief of the island, the *tulefale,* or orator. He made a great pretence that our visit was unexpected and led us to the open-sided, palm-thatched meeting house that stood on a greensward looking over the little harbour. Almost immediately, two other men appeared, looking like a South Sea version of Don Quixote and Sancho Panza. The gaunt Don was the *ali'i,* or hereditary chief, of the island; fat Sancho was the local pastor.

We were welcomed with green coconuts and introduced by Afamasaga with suitably flattering titles; I was *tusitala,* the taleteller, in memory of the much-revered Robert Louis Stevenson. Then the two chiefs slipped away, returning with twisted, grey roots of the kava plant, which they offered us as tokens of peace. There followed the traditional ceremony of the preparation and partaking of kava as a sacred and mildly narcotic drink; and a round of bombastic oratory in which I was helped by the posthumous example of the Welsh preacher uncles of my childhood; and finally a traditional island feast, borne in by a long file of youths and maidens carrying all the Polynesian delicacies of sea and land.

I was anxious to find out how the most traditional community I had yet encountered in the Polynesian world actually worked, how the apparently complete acceptance of a rather evangelical kind of Christianity was reconciled with an equally strong adherence to *fa'a Samoa,* the perpetuation in the modern world of the Samoan way of life.

The chiefs and the pastor were equally intent on finding what advantage might be reaped from this windfall visit of a *palangi* (the customary local term for a white man, which literally means heaven-breaker), whose power, thanks to Afamasaga's flowery introduction, they imagined to be great and far-reaching.

The chiefs suggested that it might be appropriate to confer on me the honorary title of *matai,* or clan chief. I had already been forewarned by a Samoan writer in Apia that I might receive such an offer, and that acquiescence would mean I would be responsible for providing benefits for my adopted community that I might not be able to afford. Afamasaga merely told me that I must be decisive one way or another; hesitation would be taken as acceptance. So I elaborately proclaimed my unworthiness, even though I already bore the revered title of tusitala.

My decision—and my gift of good silver Australian dollars and a large tin of *pisupo* (corned beef)—were accepted with sangfroid. This was still my island and my village, the tulefale assured me; I would always be welcome back—and if I could get them a new power boat and a short-wave radio, it would be appreciated.

While all this was going on, there had been a great shouting of children from the beach. We all rose and went to look in the harbour, where a high wave had come sweeping over the reef, lifting our boat so that it lay on the beach, broadside and tilting. It was soon righted, but the skipper came to tell us that we should not be too late in leaving, for the wind was beating up in the channel between Apolima and Upolu.

But the orations and the tea drinking, the appreciative smoking of our cigarettes and the gift giving could not be interrupted. And Afamasaga had to do at least a routine school inspection to justify his trip officially. The skipper came back to say we really must leave; further delay would be dangerous. But more green coconuts had to be drunk, the final speeches made, the last gifts pressed to the brow before baskets of breadfruit and coconuts were put on board and the tulefale and the young men of the village waded into the harbour to bid us farewell. The pastor had decided to accompany us to the main island, and a couple of women came as well with baskets of gifts for their relatives.

We shot the reef in great style, but the boatmen had been right in their warnings. The risk was great, and the fear slow and cumulative. The swell rose high, and the old and open boat was rolled like a shell on a beach—sometimes shuddering, through all its fragile timbers, under the impact of a wave; sometimes rising before a crest like the boat in Hokusai's famous print and scudding down sickeningly into the trough. Many times we shipped water, and the boatmen bailed steadily most of the way. I felt that any moment we would be swamped or capsized or that the boat would merely break apart in the heavy waters, and so did Inge. We did not talk of our fears until we reached dry land but, silently and almost like automatons, we exchanged things, Inge giving me my passport, which she had been carrying; I passing money to her, so that if only one survived, he or she should not be stranded.

Even Afamasaga looked grave, which perturbed me in a man who knew these waters. The pastor closed his eyes and began to mutter prayers, and the women followed his example. One of them whimpered. But I did not begin to feel fear rising to panic until I looked at the dark hand with which Afamasaga was holding one of the upright struts of the awning and saw it was so tightly clenched that it was turning white.

But we did not drown; and eventually our boat slid into the calm waters of the great lagoon of Upolu, where the waters were calm. Yet I felt nearer to death on that journey than on any other, perhaps because the fear was so prolonged, and therefore, despite the delights that accompanied the terror, I regard it as the worst of my worse journeys. But not the worst journey. That is yet to come: the journey, like Scott's, that ends in death. I have dreamed of it, but obviously not experienced it. Yet, like all true travellers, I look forward to it. Since I have to depart this earth, I would sooner do it, like Ulysses in Tennyson's poem, sailing "beyond the sunset, and the baths/Of all the western stars, until I die." Such a worst journey might also be the best.

First Foreign Lands

1993

IF I WAS not born to travel, I was certainly bred to it. When I was six months old my mother left Canada, where I had been born in Winnipeg, and took me home to that charming little manorial town, Market Drayton, our hometown in the wheat-and-cheese red sandstone country where Shropshire borders onto both Cheshire and Staffordshire. I developed early a love for wildflowers and butterflies and birds, and by the time I was nine my father was buying me W. H. Hudson's books on British birds, and then Hudson's and R. B. Cunninghame Grahame's books on the pampas and Patagonia, and afterwards the great travel narratives of the nineteenth-century wandering naturalists: Darwin on the *Beagle,* Thomas Belt on Nicaragua, A. R. Wallace on the Rio Negro and, best of all, Henry Walter Bates—*The Naturalist on the River Amazons.* These writers suddenly expanded my geographical horizons, but most lastingly they gave me a model of narrative and descriptive prose I have used ever since. It was the prose developed by John Dryden's committee of the Royal Society in the 1660s, aimed at clearing English writing of its Jacobean extravagances and making it a vehicle of direct expression. Scientists have since lost that art and write with the same dull obscurity as other scholars, but they kept it well into the nineteenth century.

I resolved to become a naturalist, not realizing that modern naturalists' lives are spent more often in laboratories than in the field. I did not succeed, in any case, because in England then the poor did not go to universities. My parents did not have enough money, and my grandfather was willing to send me to Cambridge only if I would bring what he thought was credit on the family by becoming an Anglican clergyman of Low Church inclination. This I refused to do. So I continued my pottering around as an amateur naturalist, going out with a flashlight to "sugar" trees for night moths, tramping to a chalk-hill valley where one field was a haunt of the rareish marbled white butterfly, seeking the tall, handsome summer snowflakes that grew in a marshy copse near the Thames, or going to pick the bee orchids that bloomed in a clearing in the beechwoods. Orchids had a fascination for boy naturalists in England because they were related to such splendid tropical species.

But I did begin to travel, even if not on the grand scale. My father had a clerical job on the Great Western Railway, and this enabled him to get several free passes a year, and so I shared my childhood between our home in Marlow on the Thames, where I went to school, and Market Drayton, where I went for the school holidays, more than three months a year, and stayed with my grandparents. It was one less mouth to feed for a while in a poor house in Marlow, and it gave my grandparents the satisfaction that I was not being brought up in the affected south of England with its drawled vowels.

It was those periods in Shropshire that gave me my first sense of living on the edge of a foreign culture. Shropshire was the country of Offa's Dyke, built by an Angle king of Mercia to keep out the Welsh, and its people were a mixture of the two races, red-cheeked Angles with intense blue eyes and butter-yellow hair appearing in the same families as North Welsh Celts with black hair and dark grey eyes. I came of a mixed family, mostly Welsh, with the English remainder diluted by the presence of a Dutch strain from a groom who came to England in William of Orange's entourage and founded a line of farm bai-

First Foreign Lands

liffs. However, though it was acknowledged later that I might be *cymri*—Welsh in an ancestral sense—I was not, like my friend Jan Morris, *cymri cymraeg,* or Welsh of the Welsh, for I had hardly more than a handful of words at my command and never had the time to learn more.

But I was aware of being on the edge of a foreign culture as I observed the Celtic faces that grew more predominant, like the lilting voices, as one went west across the marches to border towns like Oswestry, where many people spoke Welsh. My father had also bought me George Borrow's highly romantic *Wild Wales,* which was largely located in the central Welsh counties of Montgomery and Merioneth across the border from Oswestry. It was a region of stone and slate quarries, sheep farms and rough mountain pasture. The people were poor, almost entirely Welsh-speaking; they were often cretinous and liable to goitre because of having grown up in limestone country. Every Michelmas Fair in Market Drayton ("Dirty Fair," as we used to call it), wild Welsh drovers would come surging over the border with their herds of shaggy cattle for sale to the cattle dealers from the Potteries and the Black Country. They were always drunk, always angry looking, always shouting in their incomprehensible language, and I was not comfortable to have them for compatriots.

However, I was able to encounter Wales and its people in other ways, for some of those railway passes were used on visits to aunts who had gravitated to Wales and married there. One lived in Bridgend, an anglified town near the southern outlet to the mining valleys; her husband was a well-known lay preacher who wandered up and down the valleys, looking like a pale-faced Gandhi and developing a *hwyl* (the celebrated preachers' peroration that was appreciated throughout southeast Wales from Monmouth to Llanelly). Another was married to a very Wellsian character who made his living at Colwyn Bay repairing and hiring out bicycles, while my aunt took in a few superior holiday-makers.

When I went to my aunt at Colwyn Bay I wandered by bus along the coast, stopping in the old Norman castle towns like Conway and Caernarvon, and I did my first bit of mountaineering in the Snowdon massif, which has in miniature all the features of the great mountain ranges—tree-bare and razor-edged ridges where the wind blows strong and cold off the Irish Sea, and turquoise lakes in volcanic hollows among the hills; there was a kind of summit with a teashop and several paths going down to various passes. I chose one that was said to be mildly perilous, and got my scare, for it lay across loose shale at a steep angle on which it was hard to keep one's footing. In the little towns here like Beddgelert and Llanberis I ate all the Welsh dishes, such as leek soup, laverbread (minced dark-green seaweed served in flat cakes) and the most tender mountain lamb I have ever tasted, cooked with the herbs of its own habitat. There were stone-built and slate-roofed villages, grey in the gloomy clefts, yet brilliant even on a dull day for their tall fuschia hedges.

In Bridgend I became more closely involved in Welsh life, drinking in pubs that were not filled with Liverpool holidaymakers as on the North Coast, going to the rugby games and taking bus and tramping trips up the coal-mining and metal-smelting valleys, with their double streets, one on each side of the same polluted river, and often double railway lines put down by rival Victorian speculators. It was Depression era, and the contrasts were often striking. You went up a valley that was uncannily silent because the machinery was not working in the deserted copper smelting and tin plating works, and the great wheels at the pitheads were motionless. The unaccustomed clearness of the air already had allowed a turf of tender green to grow over the recently bare hillsides. As the old men would say to me: "We're getting clear water and clear air again after a long time, and there's lovely that is, boyo, but we still need the cash we haven't got. *Ach y fi,* it's a hard time." And as likely as not men would be squatting around us on a waste lot, playing the miner's idle-hour game, pitch-and-toss, but with flat stones or buttons because they had no pennies.

I talked to people in the streets, in the poorly attended pubs, in little Italian cafés collectively named Bracchi, on the buses and once or twice as they were picking wretched fragments of coal off the colliery slag heaps. Some of the men had been out of

First Foreign Lands

work for almost a decade, and I was impressed by their fortitude and their courtesy to strangers like me. The miners here all talked an accented English with its own strange expressions, and among themselves they spoke not the pure Welsh of—say —Carmarthen or Cardigan, but a macaronic lingo, Welsh with English words incorporated. There was not all that much nationalism around in those days, except in the Anglicized cities like Cardiff and Swansea, for then the grievances were economic, and a politically minded (often Communist) miner in Tonypandy felt more in common with a politically minded (often Communist) unemployed shipbuilder in the Gorbals than with the schoolmasters and postal clerks and drapers' clerks who then made up the nationalist banner.

Still, a great deal of ethnic feeling went into their choral singing, for which I loved rugby games and miners' funerals, when *Cwm Rhondda* would boom out over the bare hillsides as the union banners slapped against the staves in the constant wind, and into the local *eisteddfodau,* the gatherings in the rural villages where the Welsh language was read and celebrated. I stayed once in such a village for a week as the guest of a local poet, reciting and reading poetry, both English and Welsh, in the local pub, *Y Ddraig Goch* (the Red Dragon), and it remains, fifty years after, the most moving literary experience of my life.

It was in Wales that I first encountered French people, other than a few waiters in Soho and the "six-penny barber" in Marlow to whom all the boys went on entering grammar school, having previously attended the "four-penny barber" with his nimble clippers in the basement of our great old coaching hotel.

The roughest part of the port at Cardiff was a place called Tiger Bay, a quarter of pubs and sailors' rooming houses that had once been notorious for all the crimping that went on there, and which in the thirties was still a "dare" to visit. When I did go I found the old wharves lined with dumpy little Breton sailing boats with vermilion sails and old hulls painted with gay but fading colours, often on their prows the magical protective eyes that Odysseus and the other ancient voyagers had on their boats, and which later I would find in the fisher craft of the Camargue, where Van Gogh painted them.

Of course, these men did not regard themselves as French except in a vague political way. Their Celtic dialects were akin to Welsh, and most of what they had to say was understood by many people in Wales. They used to wander off up the valleys, dressed in their black berets, their black corduroy jackets and trousers, and go from door to door with plaits of large onions hanging from their shoulders. They were always welcome and earned quite a lot of money; the Welsh called them, collectively, Shoni Onion.

In 1935 I went to France for the first time, with my wretched grammar-school French and a longing to enter a different world. And a far different world it was then than it is now, since the homogenizing influence of American civilization has destroyed the free old Parisian life, destroyed it not only by homogenization but also by pollution, by recurrent bouts of that typical French fever, excessive bureaucratization, complicated by an unexpected rise of Jansenist puritanism. For all its grossness and callousness towards the unfortunate, La Belle Époque had been a time when the arts of pen and brush, of music and dance, flourished in a freedom that extended into lifestyles and produced its own willing restraints. I was fortunate to arrive when some of the atmosphere and achievement of the époque survived; it was, after all, still Picasso's and Gide's Paris; Proust was only recently dead, Jean Cocteau was still camping it high, and if I had known it I could have got into Gertrude Stein's salon by giving a pound of coffee to Alice B. Toklas, as the custom still was.

I stayed that first time in a clean, meagre little hotel near the Madeleine, on the right bank, which for me was the wrong bank, for I soon discovered that apart from a visibly decaying Montmartre, bohemian Paris, insofar as it survived, was to be found in the narrow, time-grimed streets of the Latin Quarter, of which the Boul' Mich' was the main thoroughfare; always, after my first visit, I stayed in this quarter. Farther south, a sharp walk away at the great crossroads of the Boulevard de Montparnasse and the Boulevard Raspail, were to be found the great arty cafés, with their crowded terraces: La Rotonde, Le Coupole, Le Select. This was always an international rather than a truly French community; the American "Lost Generation," together with sundry Canadian hangers-on like Morley Callaghan and Buffy Glassco, made it their stamping ground. By 1935 the Depression had already thinned the American contingent, and it was just as often Swedes or Swiss, Germans or Dutch, though rarely French, that one drank with so deeply and so cheaply in the bars of Montparnasse, which were even cheaper than the terrasses.

Indeed, apart from the sense of liberation, the great attraction of France in those days was its cheapness. "Das ist billig, das muss man sagen," the Germans would remark, and it was true, with a fiver in one's pocket, or say $25, one could live a week there in style, with a small but clean hotel room, prix fixe lunches in the student quarter, a slap-up six-course dinner every other night, lots to drink, all one's bus and Métro travel, a day's side trip to Fountainebleau or Rambouillet, and a couple of visits to burlesque or theatre or opera.

Even if I have never learnt to like the Parisians over my many trips to the city (I found their linguistic snobbery impossible), yet I was better off than the Québecois whose accents they seemed to treat with total contempt. And I still found the city and the way of life they had created over almost a millenium delightful and liberating. It began with the physical atmosphere, the streets bathed in warm sunlight as one stepped out of the Gare St. Lazare, and the air—cleansed by the great parks and the treed boulevards, and both light and fragrant, for from spring to autumn there was always something blooming abundantly.

All that, of course, changed in the early fifties with the spread of the automobile, and it is many years since the stench of badly refined French gasoline drove me from the pleasure of taking a coffee or a *fine* or a *Vermouth Cassis* on a Paris café terrasse and just watching the sheer variety of humanity.

And then there was the moral freedom. Mme. Richard, the terrible reforming lady, had not yet materialized, and great rococo brothels like the Sphinx still flourished on the appropriately named Rue de la Gaîté, where there were freely operating clubs to suit all diverse tastes. Bars and cafés stayed open as long as their proprietors wished, and yet one saw fewer drunks than in London with its restricted opening hours. Liberty, as always, had created its own discipline. With a whole evening, a whole night before one, there was not the urgent need to have just one more before the barman called, "Time, gentlemen, please." The great galleries with their masterpieces of old and modern art were endlessly fascinating, the old churches were treasure houses of mediaeval antiquity, and the bookshops and stalls in the little streets of the Latin Quarter and along the Seine filled one's days with interest.

And then there was the burgeoning political excitement of the times, the great stay-in strikes and the heroic rumour of the Spanish Civil War that dominated the great Bastille Day marches on whose verges I tramped, triumphal in 1936, still hopeful in 1937 and threnodic by 1938. I got my first sense of the meaning of anarchism then, and it was in 1938 or perhaps in 1939 that I was on the edge of being arrested by the police of the Sûreté because I turned up with a letter from the left socialist Frank Ridley to the head of a small radical faction whose office was just being raided and sealed. An act of gormlessness and my French, more than usually bad that day, saved me from the *panier de salade,* though I was tailed for the rest of the day.

I had already begun to consider myself an adoptive Parisian and might never have gone beyond if the French railways had not offered free passes in 1939 to English railway workers. Possibility stirred my curiosity and I decided to spend a few days in Provence that year. It took me a day to travel from Paris through Burgundy to Arles. By the time I got there I was fascinated by what I had seen—the banks of the Rhône covered with green-blue vineyards; the Papal Palace at Avignon and the great Roman arch of Orange and the old castle of Tarascon over the rooftops, and as night fell the contorted black trunks of the olive trees and their strange greyish foliage dramatically lit by a full moon. In Arles I drove along narrow crowded streets, with the people's faces almost against the taxi window, to the old Nord Pinus Hotel, with a trio of Roman columns and part of the great architrave built into its façade on the old Forum.

Now I was at last on the verge of the real foreign travel in which I later spent so much of my time, on the verge of alien cultures and even of the archaic world, for it was in the sixth century B.C. that the Phocaeans, the people of the City of Seals, had fled en masse from Ionia and founded Marseilles, from which half the cities of the Alpes Maritimes sprouted—Nice and Antibes, St. Rémy and Arles itself, where the superstructure might be Roman but the foundation was Greek. It was the Greeks who voyaged up the Rhône, taking their artifacts to the Celtic chiefs and introducing the culture of the grape and the olive. And the Greco-Roman buildings, like the great amphitheatre at Arles and the Maison Carrée at Nîmes and the Pont du Gard, were still being used, retained in twentieth-century society. Van Gogh fields and olive groves and almond orchards and fishing boats were still there, in the colours Vincent had painted them. The sunlit hills covered with wild lavender and purple rock roses and mimosa and sometimes impenetrable maquis were a world of their own, of strange insects and birds and reptiles, where Fabre had made his famous studies. The people —speakers of the langue d'oc still in many places—were not arrogant North Sea folk like the Parisians but laid-back Mediterranean people merging towards the Italian on the east and the Spanish on the west and including already many North Africans. A memory of courtly poetry still hung in the air, and a memory of the gentle and cruelly suppressed Gnostic heresy, Catharism. A different people, a different world. I would have stayed longer if the war had not threatened, but the taste of the world's possibilities was what made me so eager after the six years of conflict to get away, first to Canada, and then to India, Egypt, Cambodia, Mexico, Persia, Peru and Lebanon, where the great sampling of various antiquities survived, and where people still often lived with growing precariousness by ancient and wise custom.

But in the six years that stretched so appallingly between 1939 and 1945, it was Wales that remained my only accessible foreign land, so that I still treasure its rhythms of speech and song, and consider myself a Welsh patriot, fervent for my people's freedom, even though I have spoken no more of the language than Dylan Thomas.

ACKNOWLEDGEMENTS

Some of the articles and essays in this collection have been previously published:

"Don Jaime's Fiesta," *The New Statesman and Nation*, 15 January 1955; "A Day to Mitla," *Northern Review*, Spring 1955; "Peru Today," *Saturday Night*, 10 November 1956; "A Road in the Andes," *Tamarack Review*, Spring 1957; "Cambodia," *Arts Magazine*, December 1964; "Letter from the Khyber Pass," *Saturday Night*, June 1965; "The Exciting Centre of the Middle East," *Saturday Night*, October 1966; "A Northern Journal," *The Beaver*, Summer 1969; "Lhasa in the Jungle," *Saturday Night*, May 1970; "Oases in a Fluid Desert," *Saturday Night*, January 1973; "Spirit Dance of the Salish People," *Saturday Night*, December 1976; "From Rotorua to Tasman Bay," *Saturday Night*, December 1979; "Lost Worlds of Memory," *Aurora: New Canadian Writing 1979*, ed. Morris Wolfe, Doubleday: 1989; "Seven Burmese Days," *Canadian Forum*, July 1983; "Encounters with India," *Quest*, October 1983; "Back to Spain," *Western Living*, May 1986; "The Caves in the Desert," *Western Living*, December 1987; "My Worst Journeys," *Bad Trips: A Sometimes Terrifying, Sometimes Hilarious Collection of Writing on the Perils of the Road*, ed. Keath Fraser, Random House: 1990.

GEORGE WOODCOCK is one of Canada's most respected men of letters. He is a biographer, critic, essayist and poet, and his more than seventy books include *Anarchism: A History of Libertarian Ideas and Movements,* a subject in which he has held a lifelong interest, *British Columbia: A History of the Province, The Doukhobors* and *The Monk and His Message.*

His biographies include *The Crystal Spirit,* about George Orwell, which won the Governor General's Award in 1967; *Gabriel Dumont,* which won the University of British Columbia Medal for Popular Biography in 1976, and *Thomas Merton: Monk and Poet.*

He was the founder and for twenty years the editor of *Canadian Literature,* and his writings on that subject include *The World of Canadian Writing: Critiques and Recollections, Strange Bedfellows: The State and the Arts in Canada* and *Northern Spring: The Flowering of Canadian Literature.*

JIM CHRISTY is the author of several books, including *Rough Road to the North* and *Travellin' Light.* He travels often, and his interests range from hagiography to pre-Columbian exploration. His most recent book is *Flesh & Blood: A Journey into the Heart of Boxing* (Douglas & McIntyre, 1990).